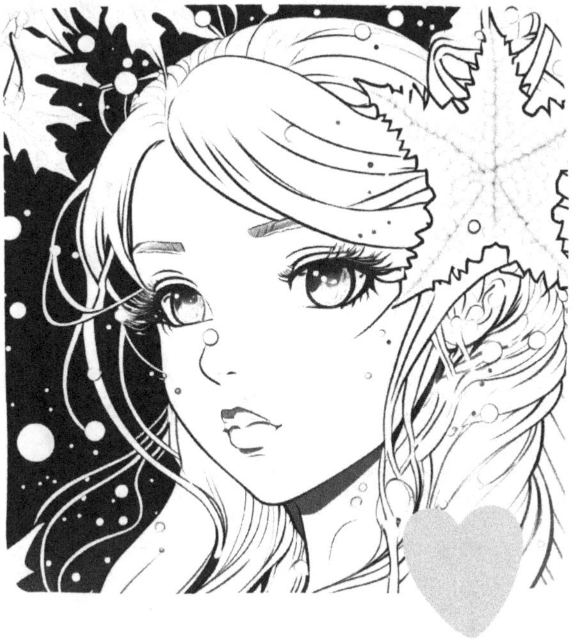

塗り絵 MORE SUPER KAWAII PRINCESSES

CAPI CAMP
ESTUDIOS

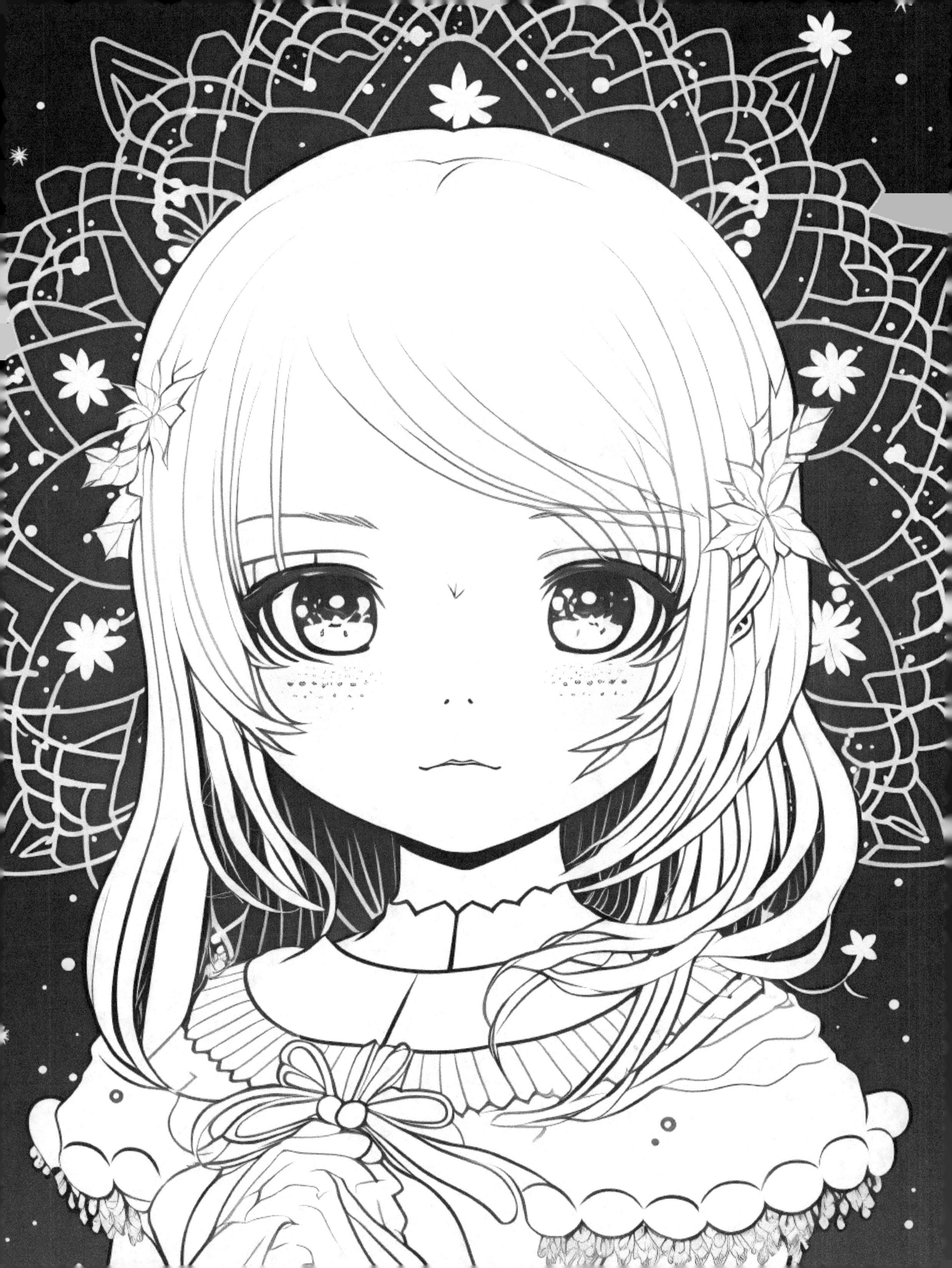

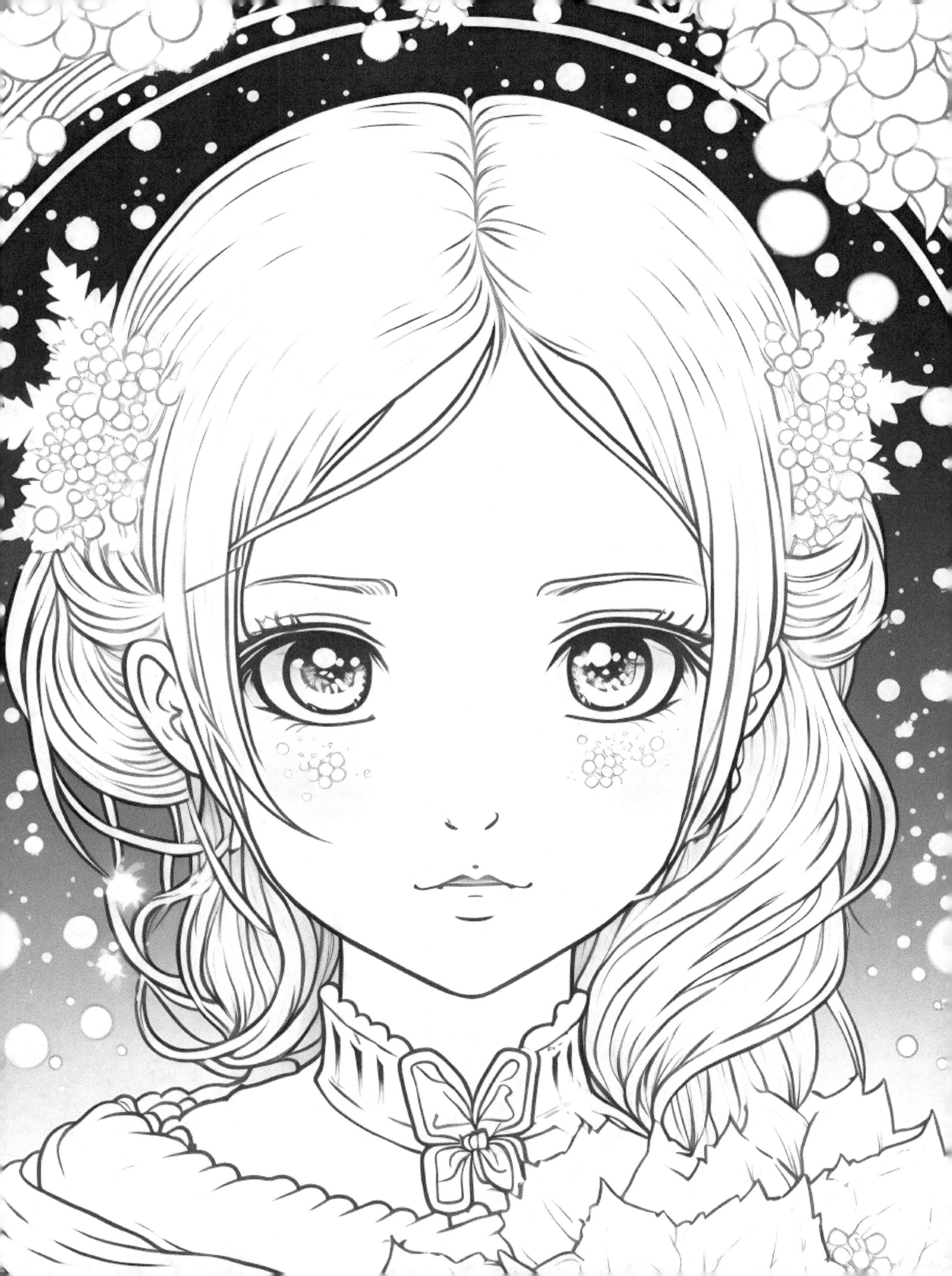

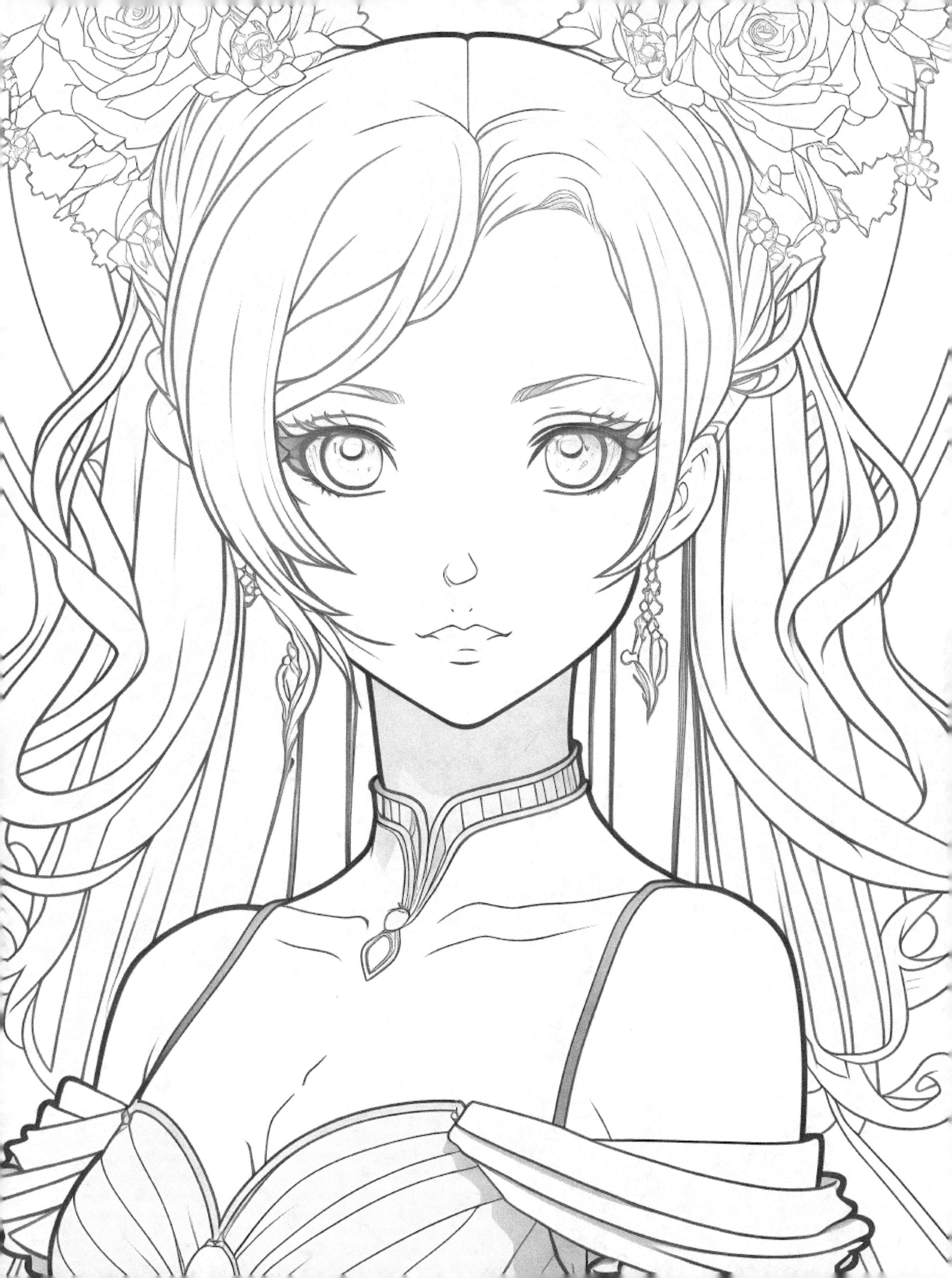

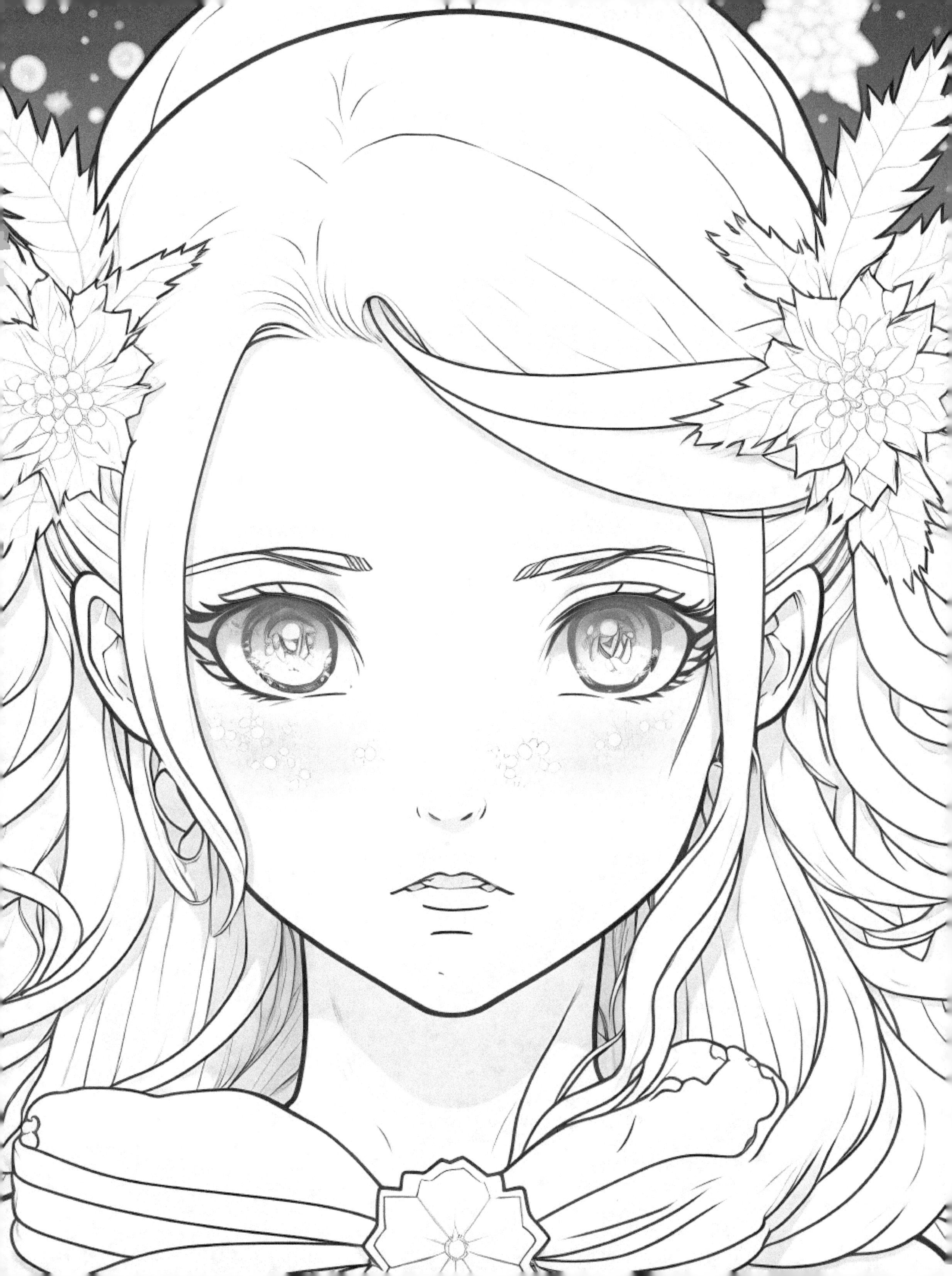

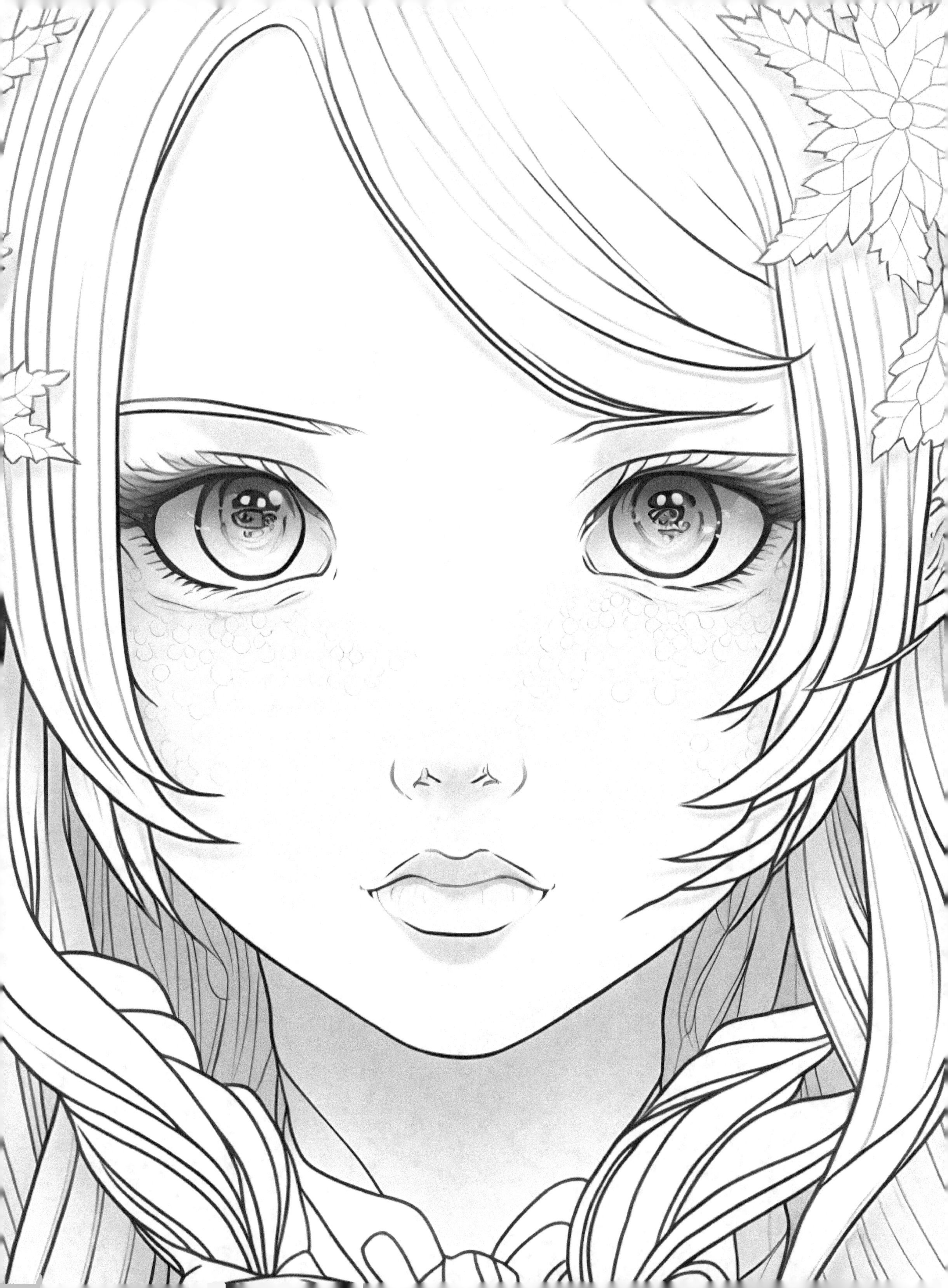

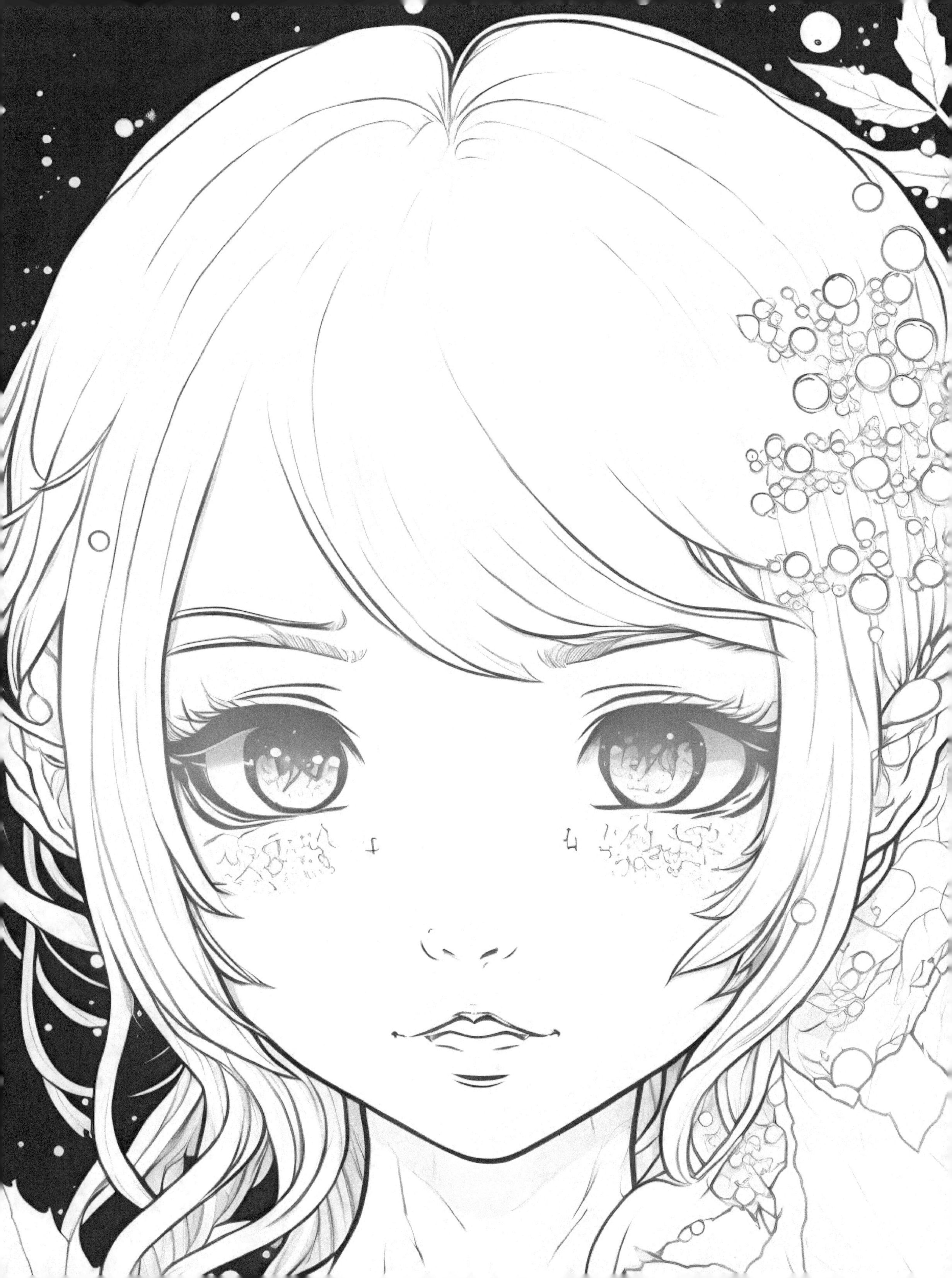

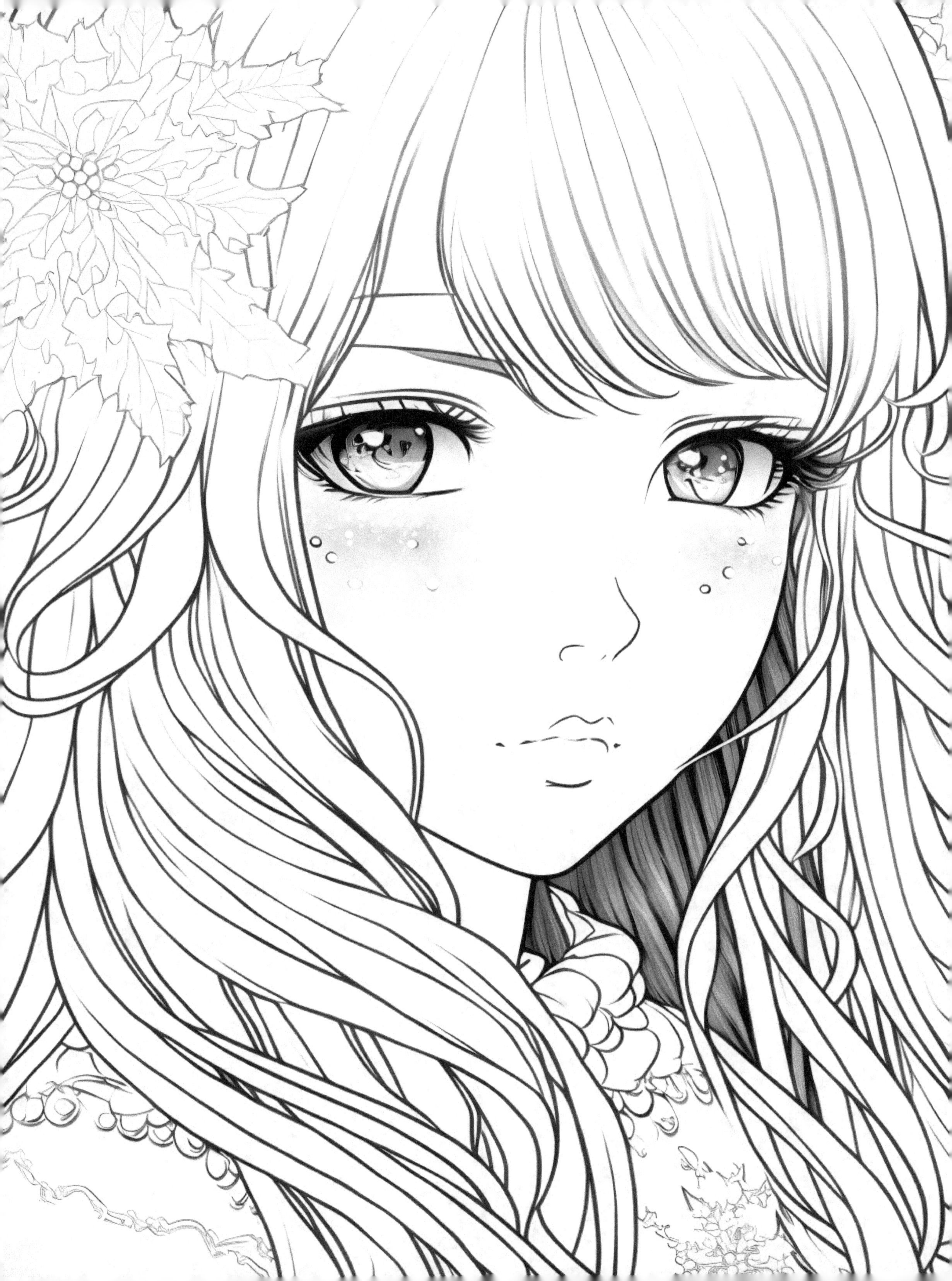

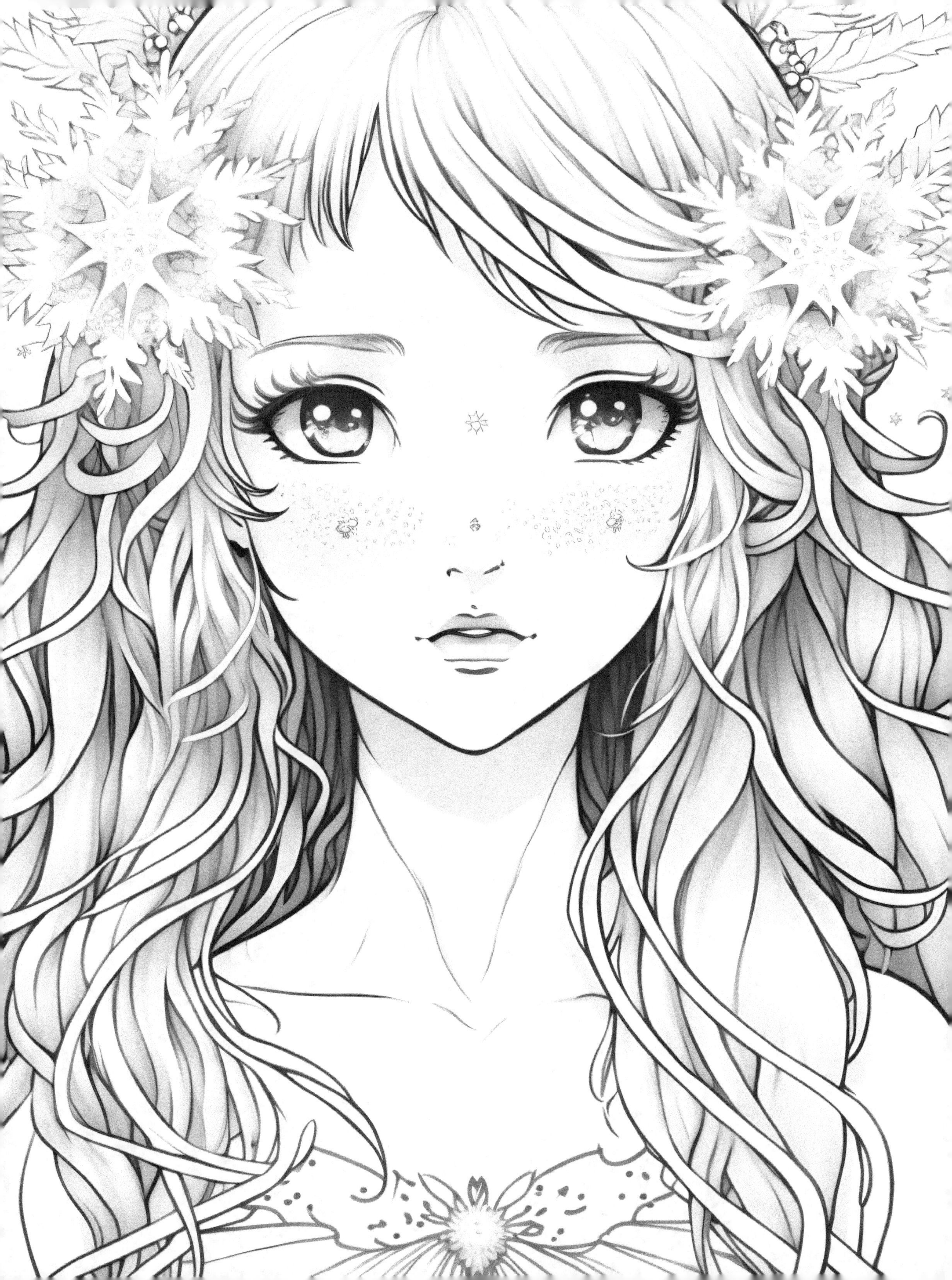

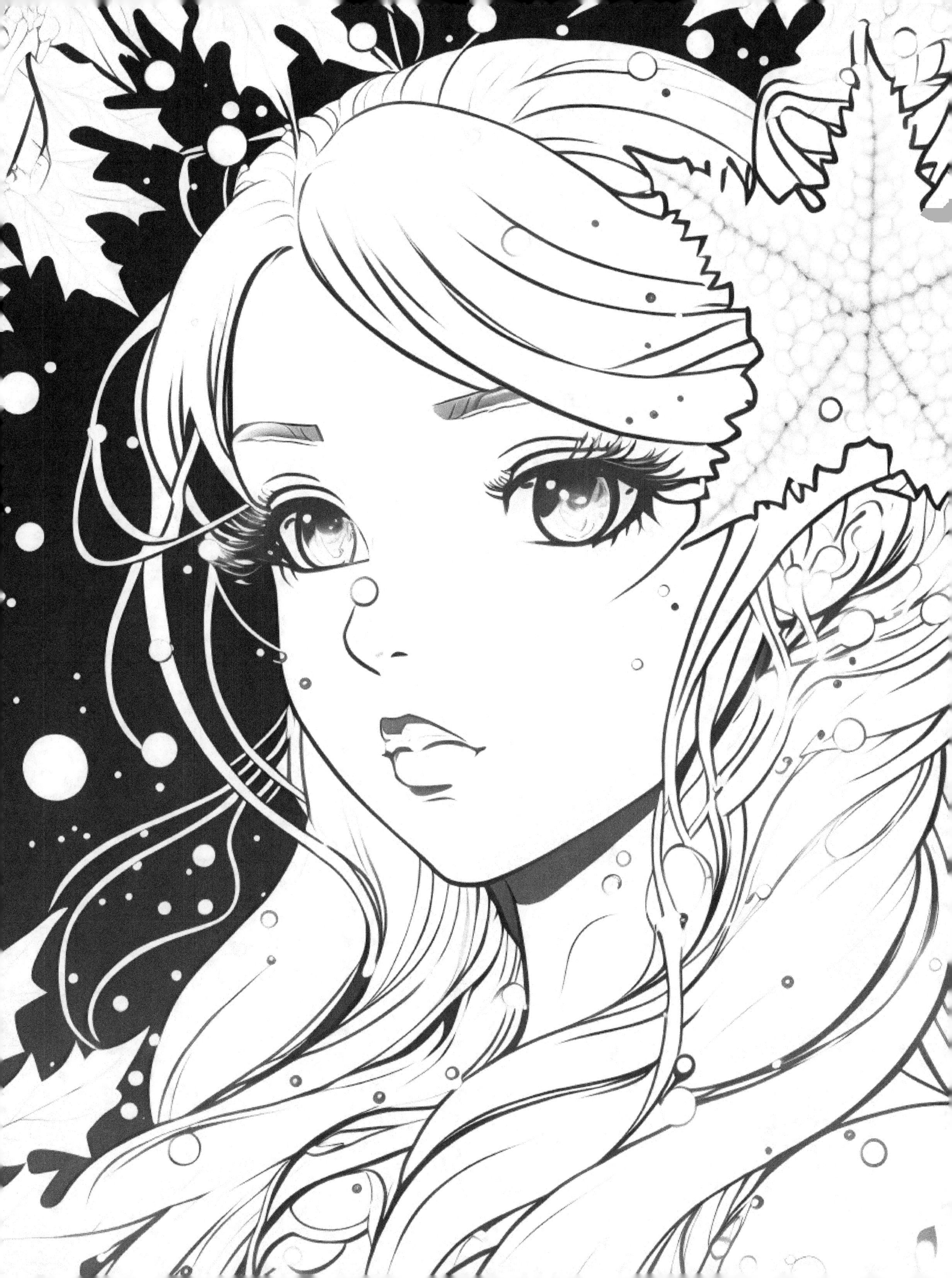

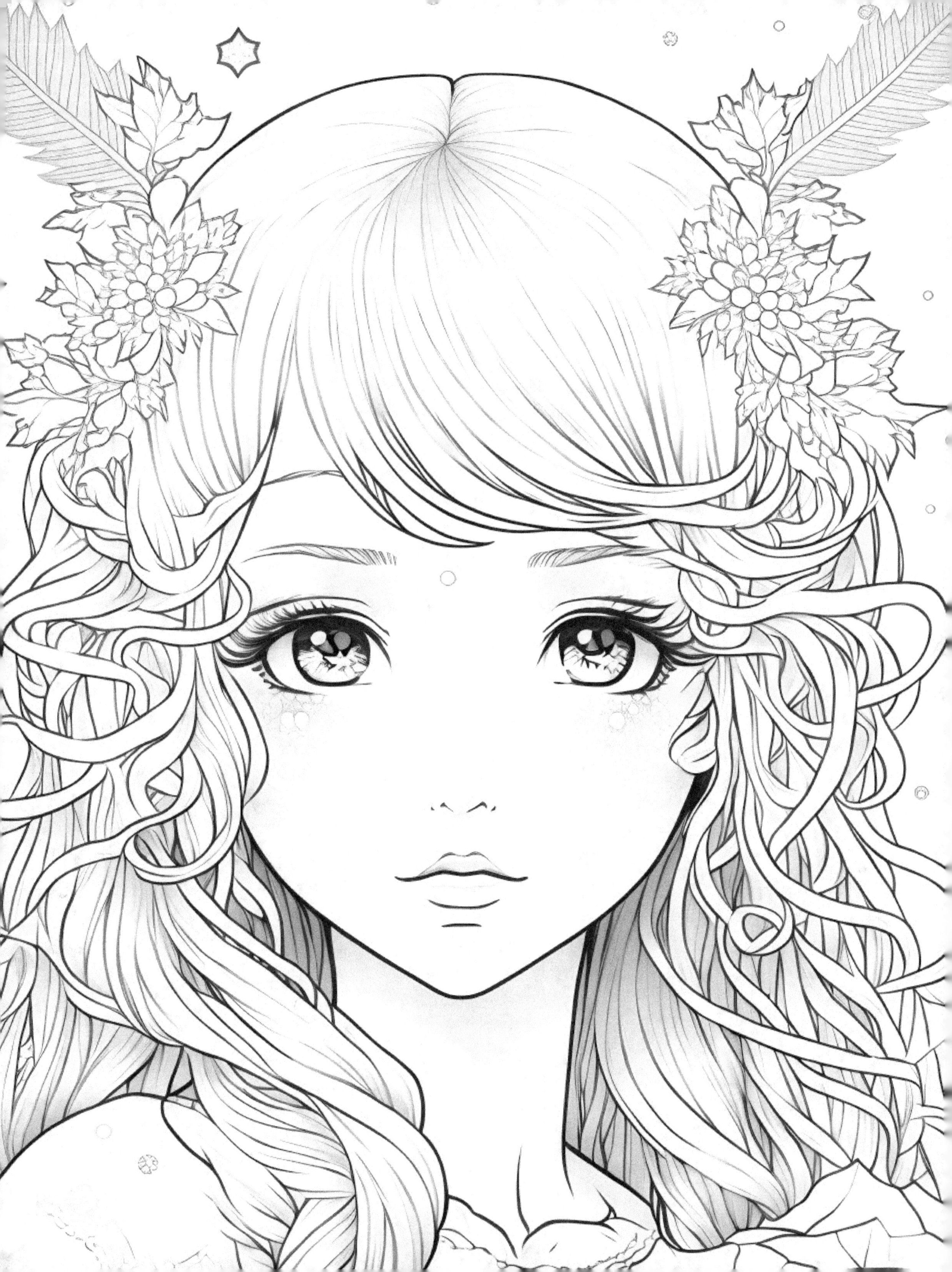

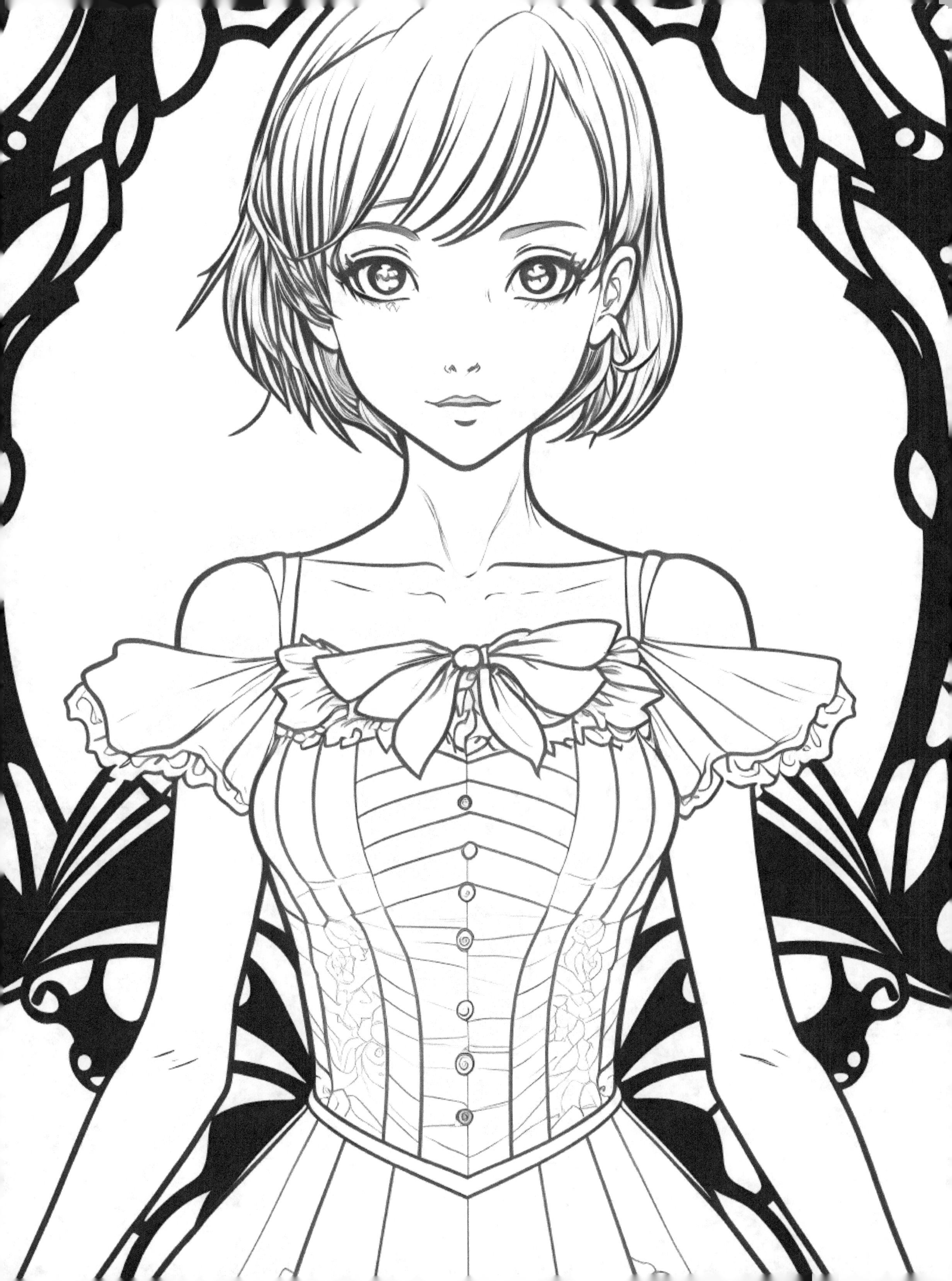

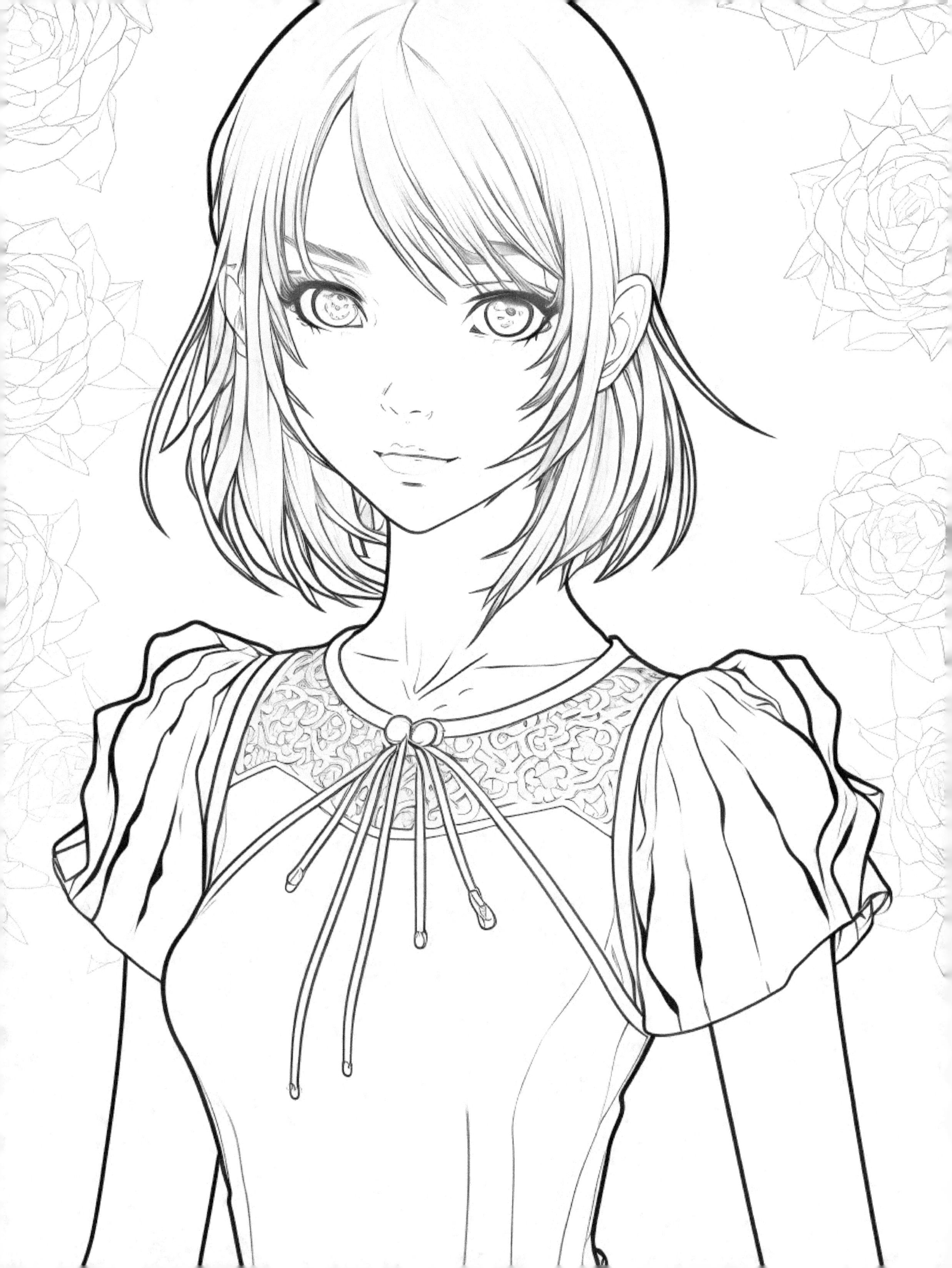

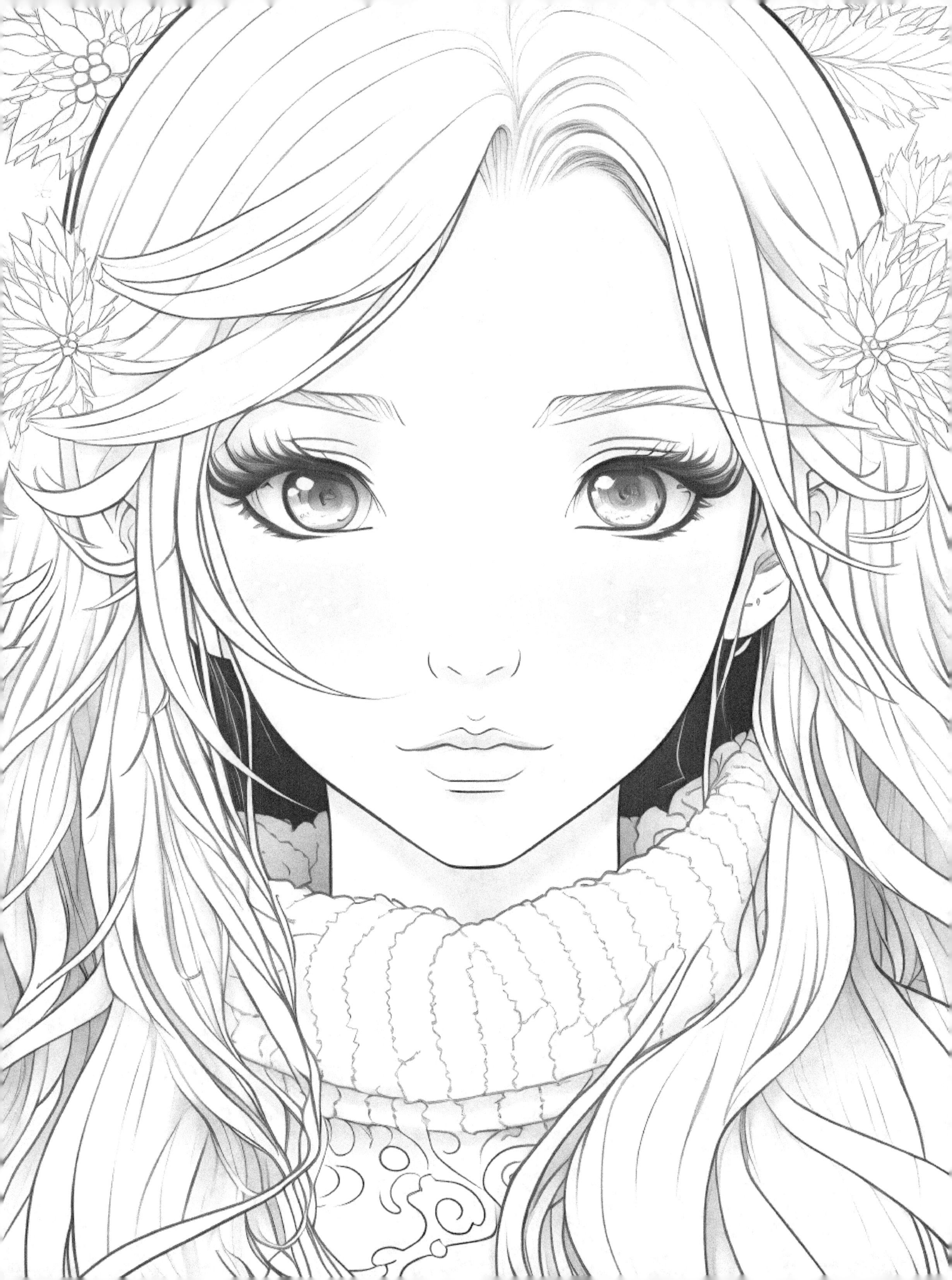

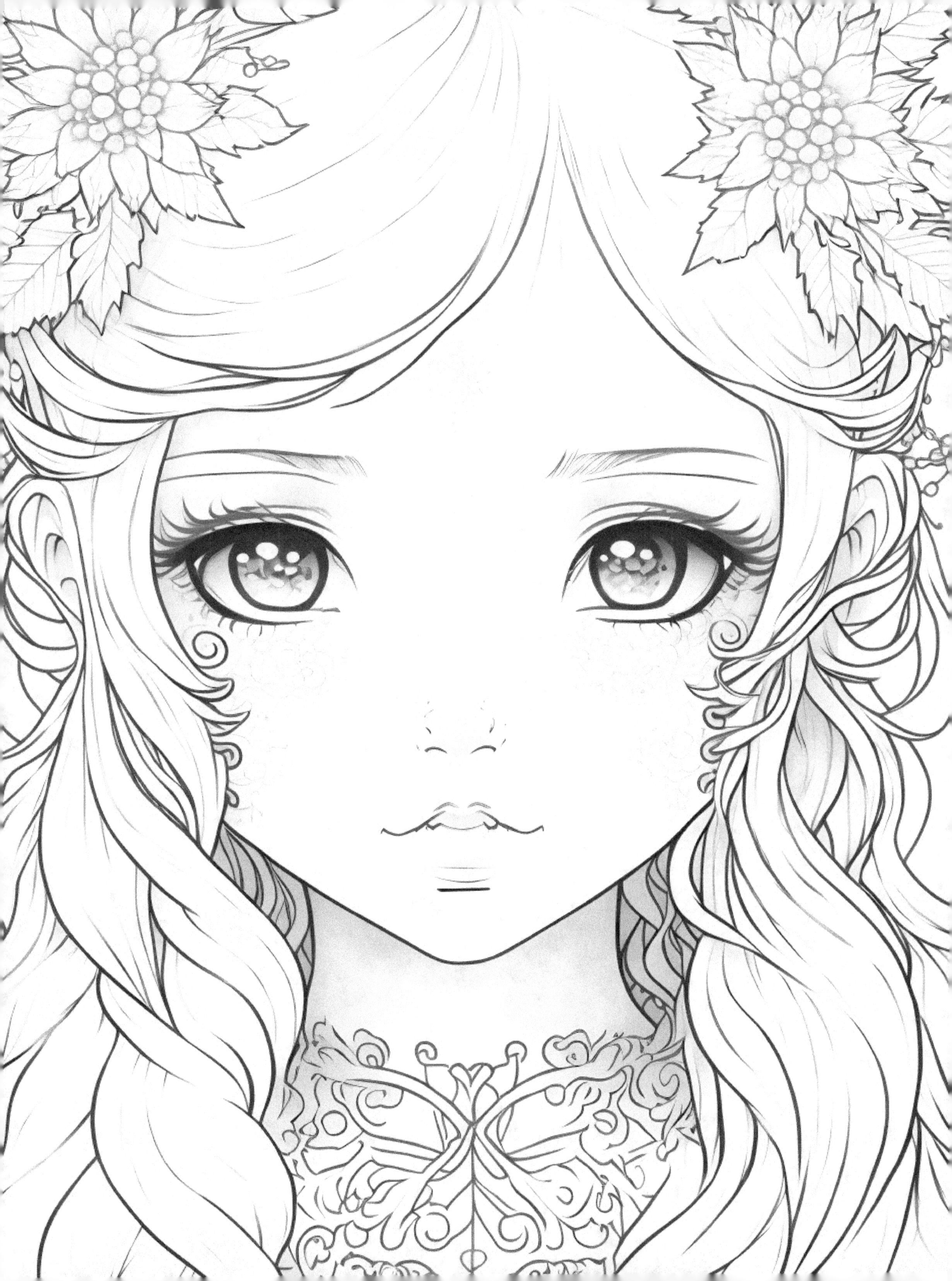

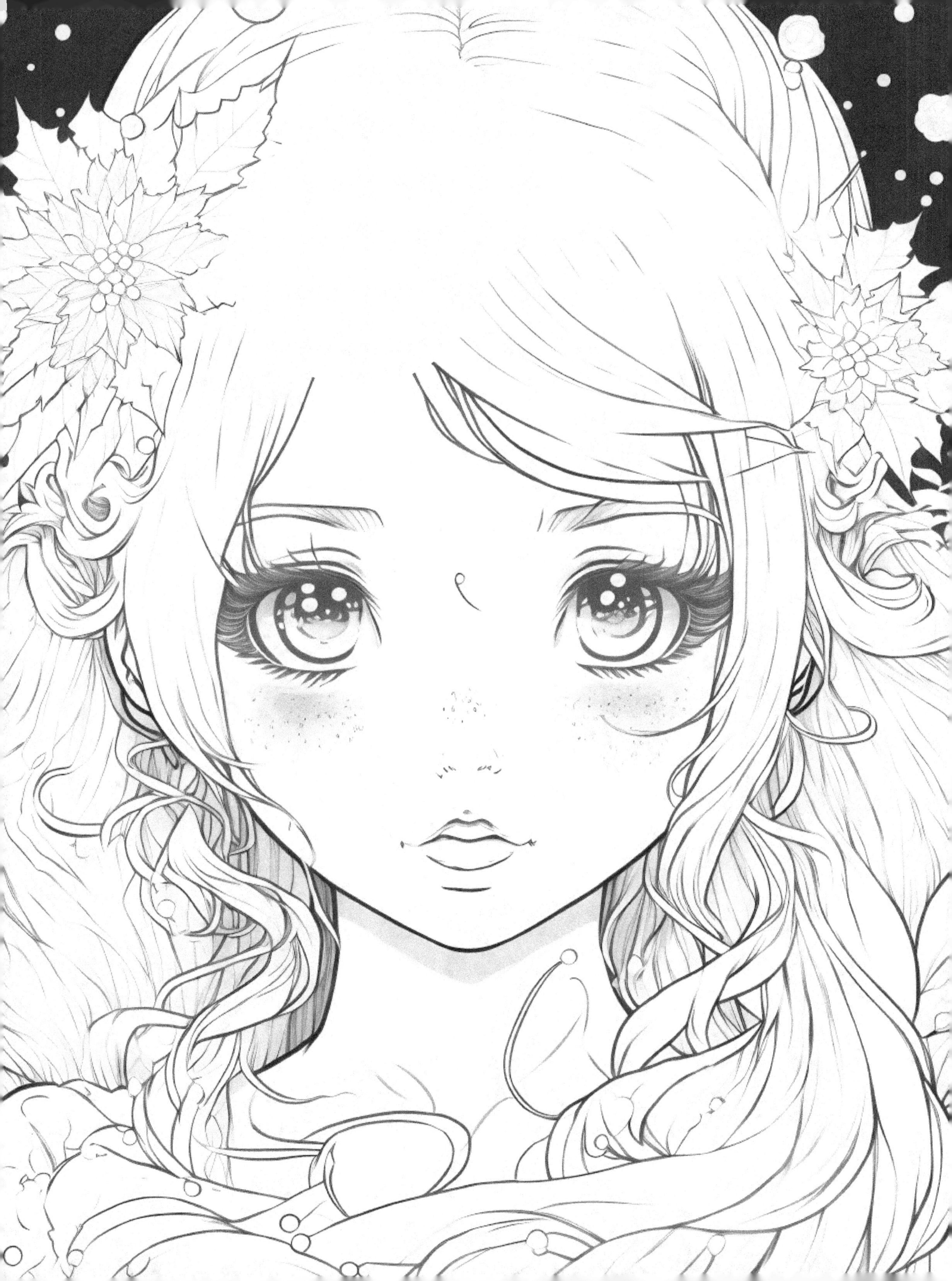

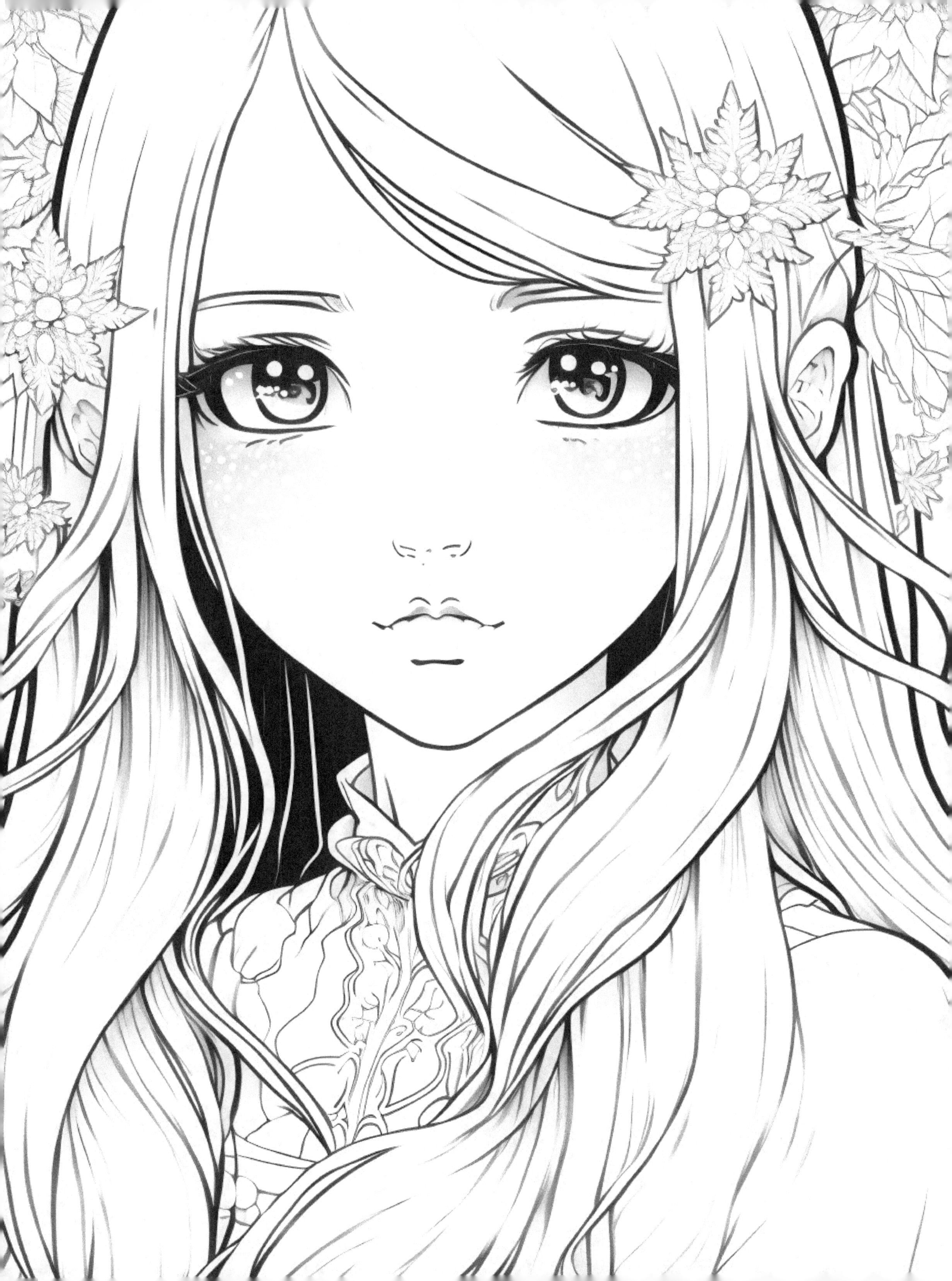

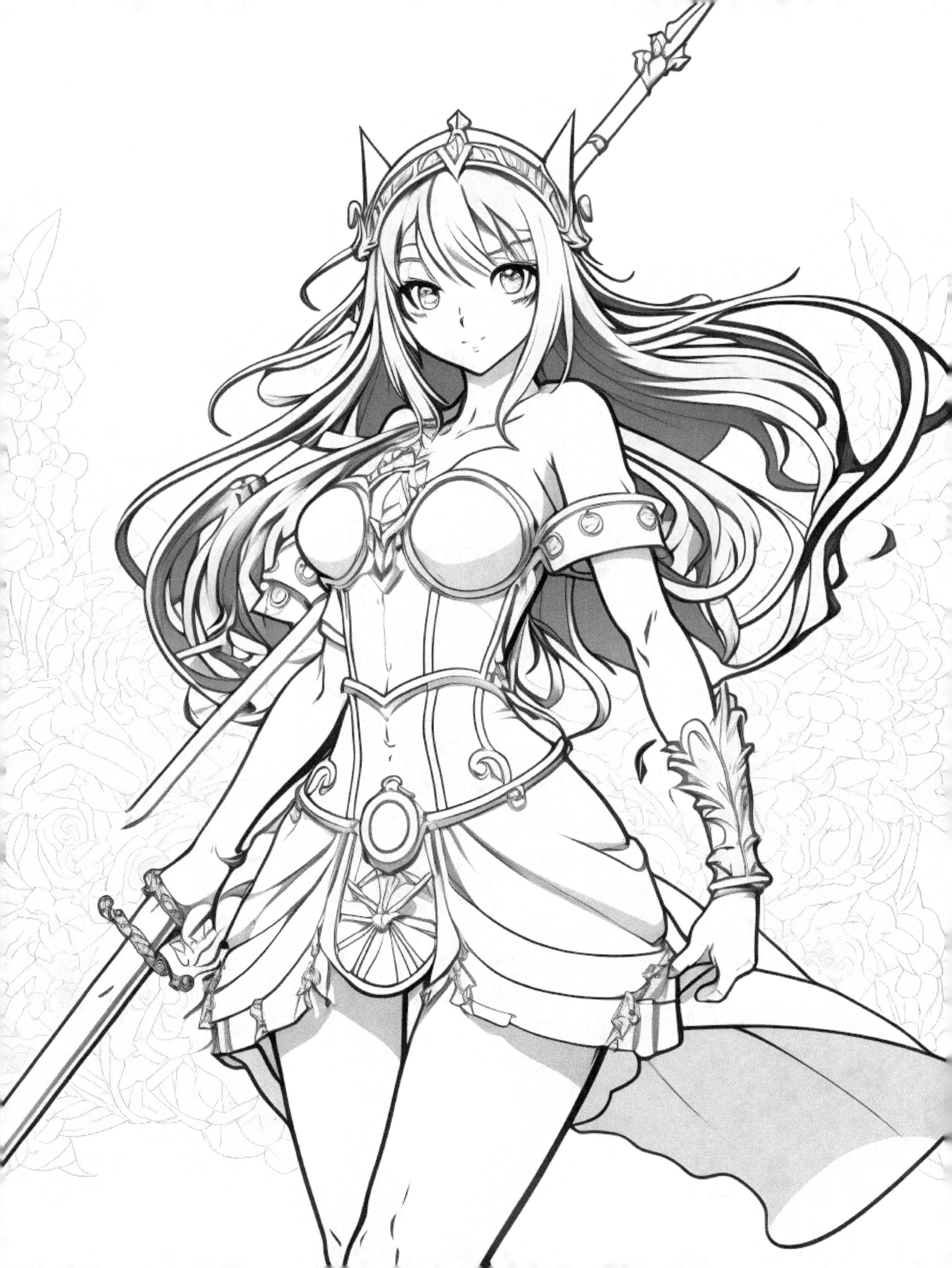

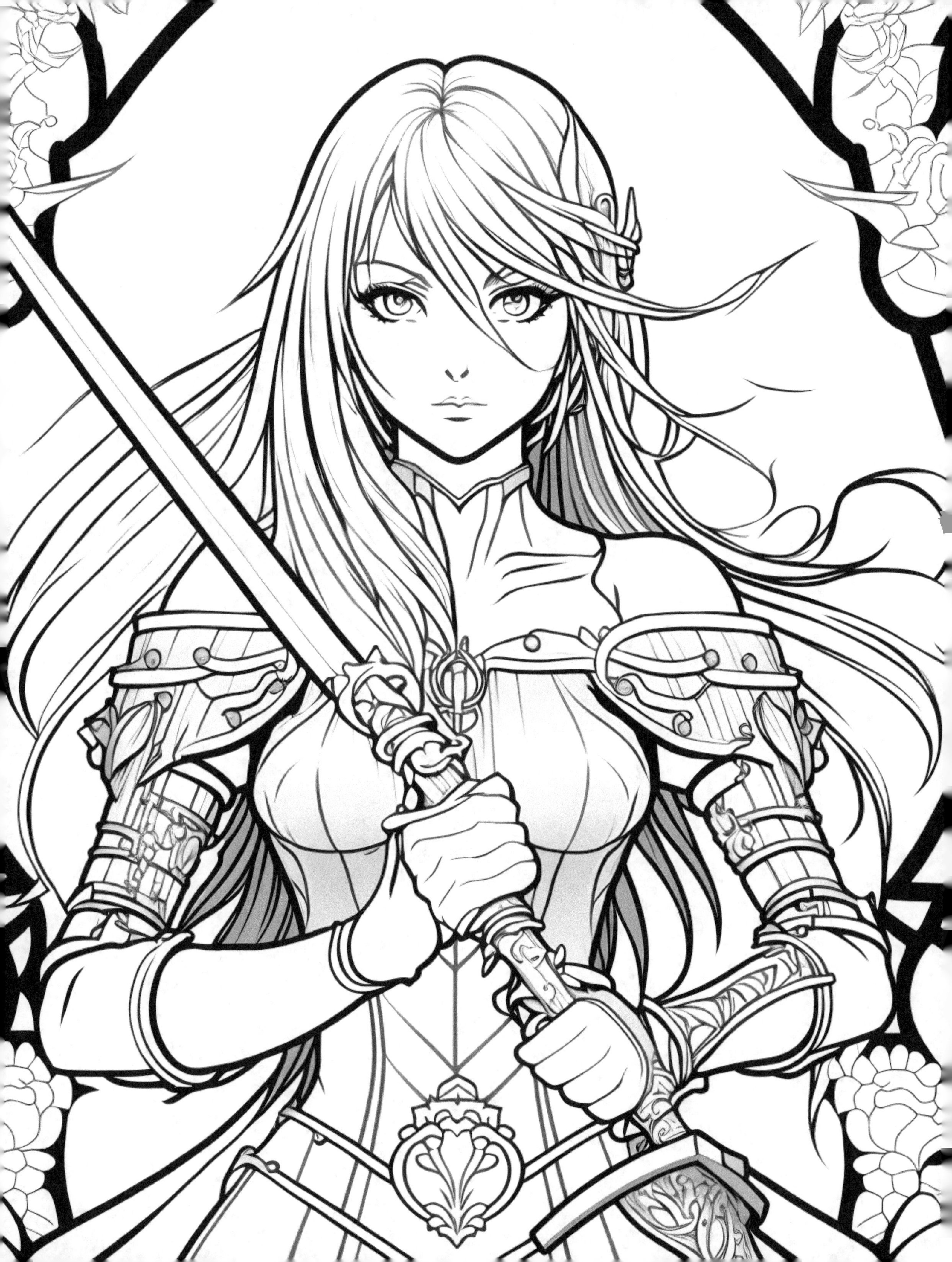

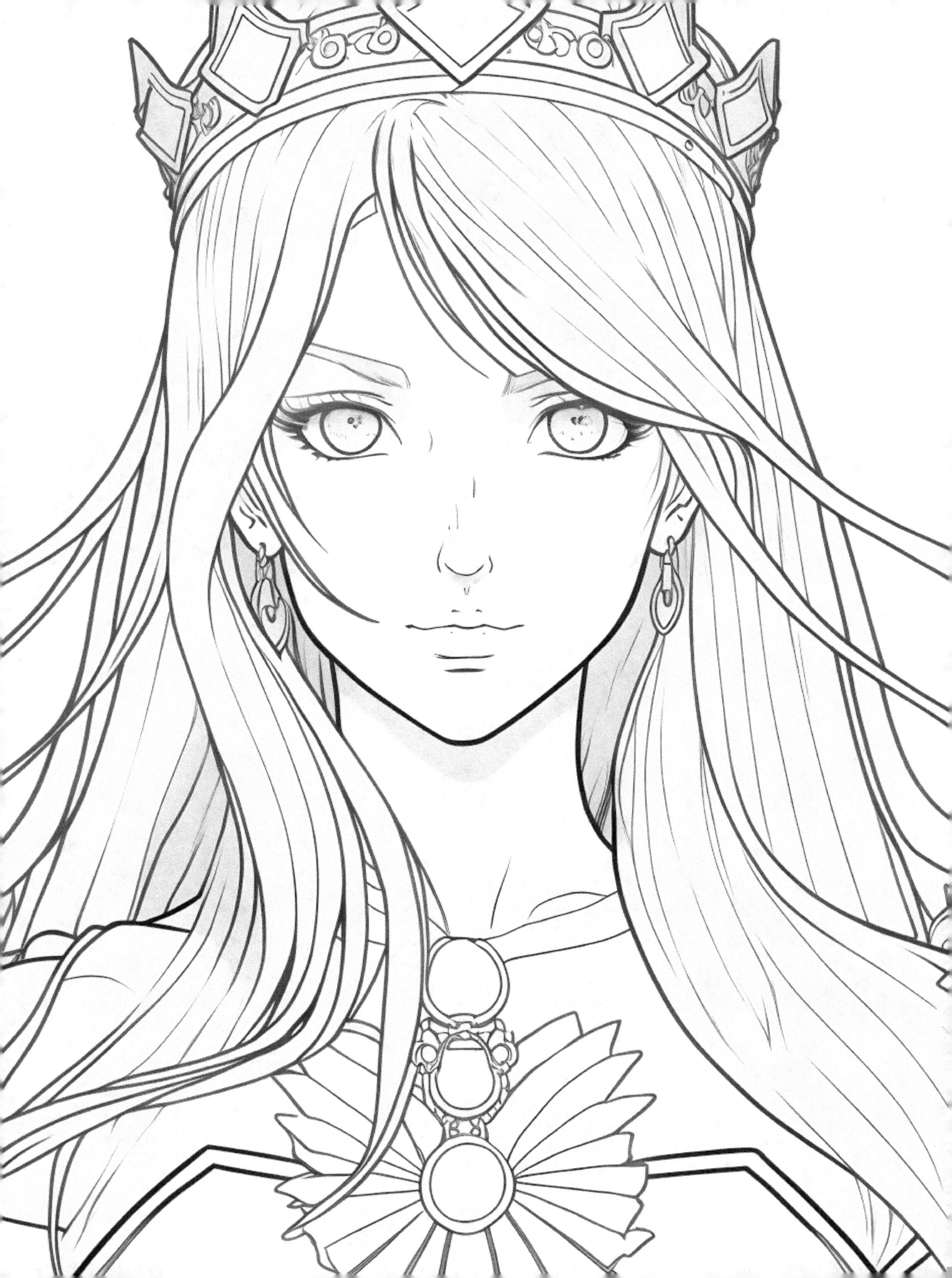

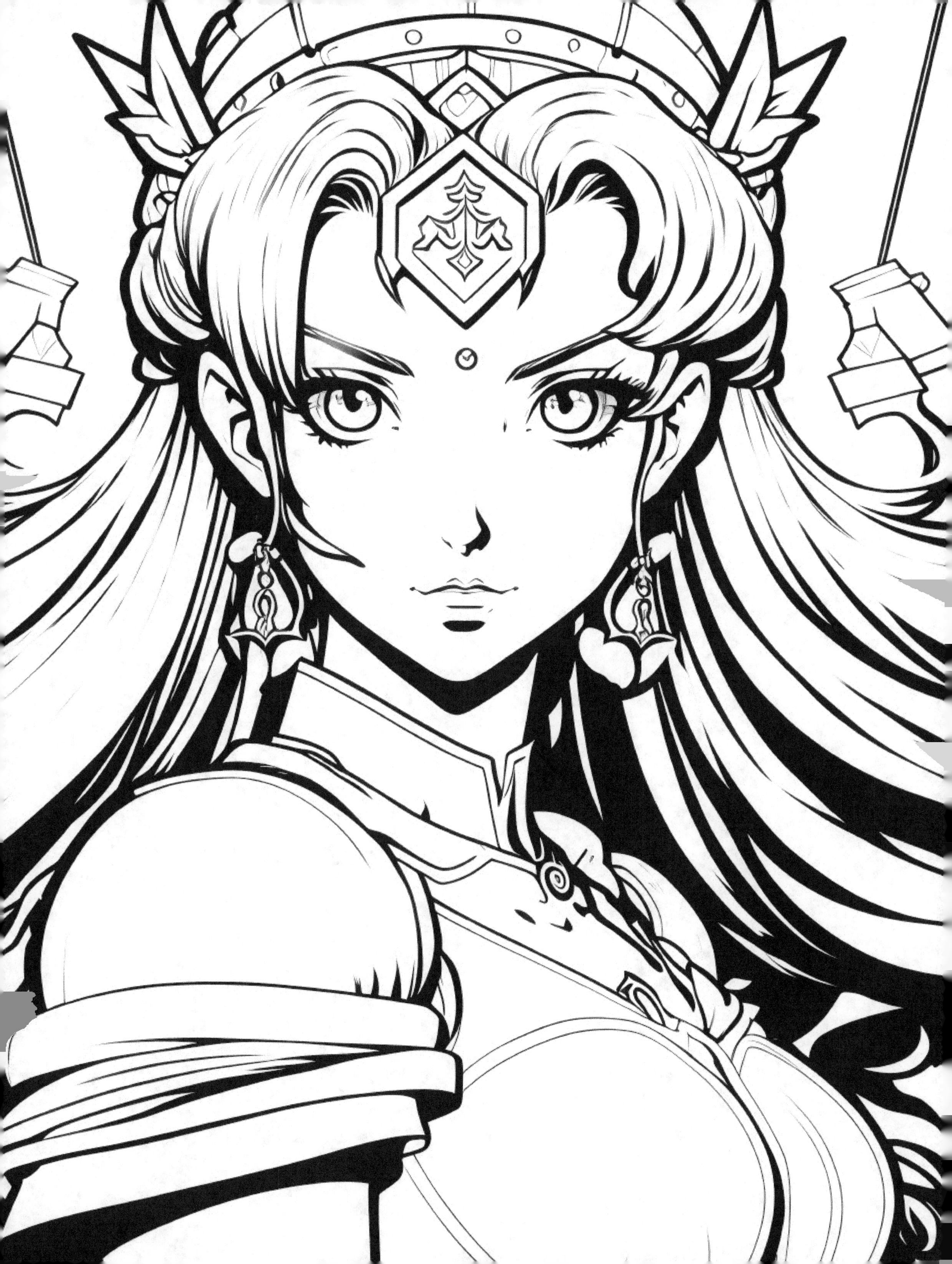

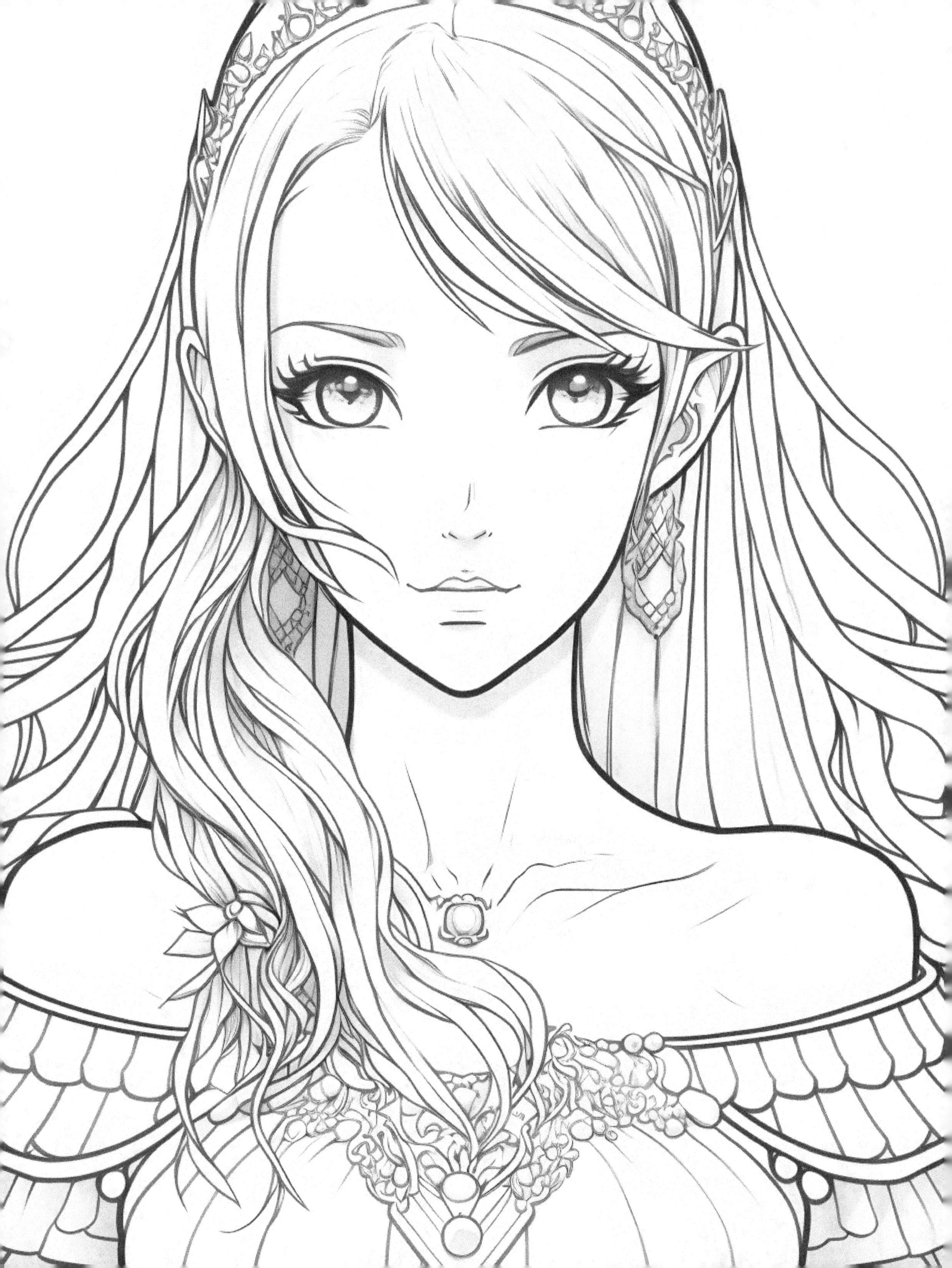

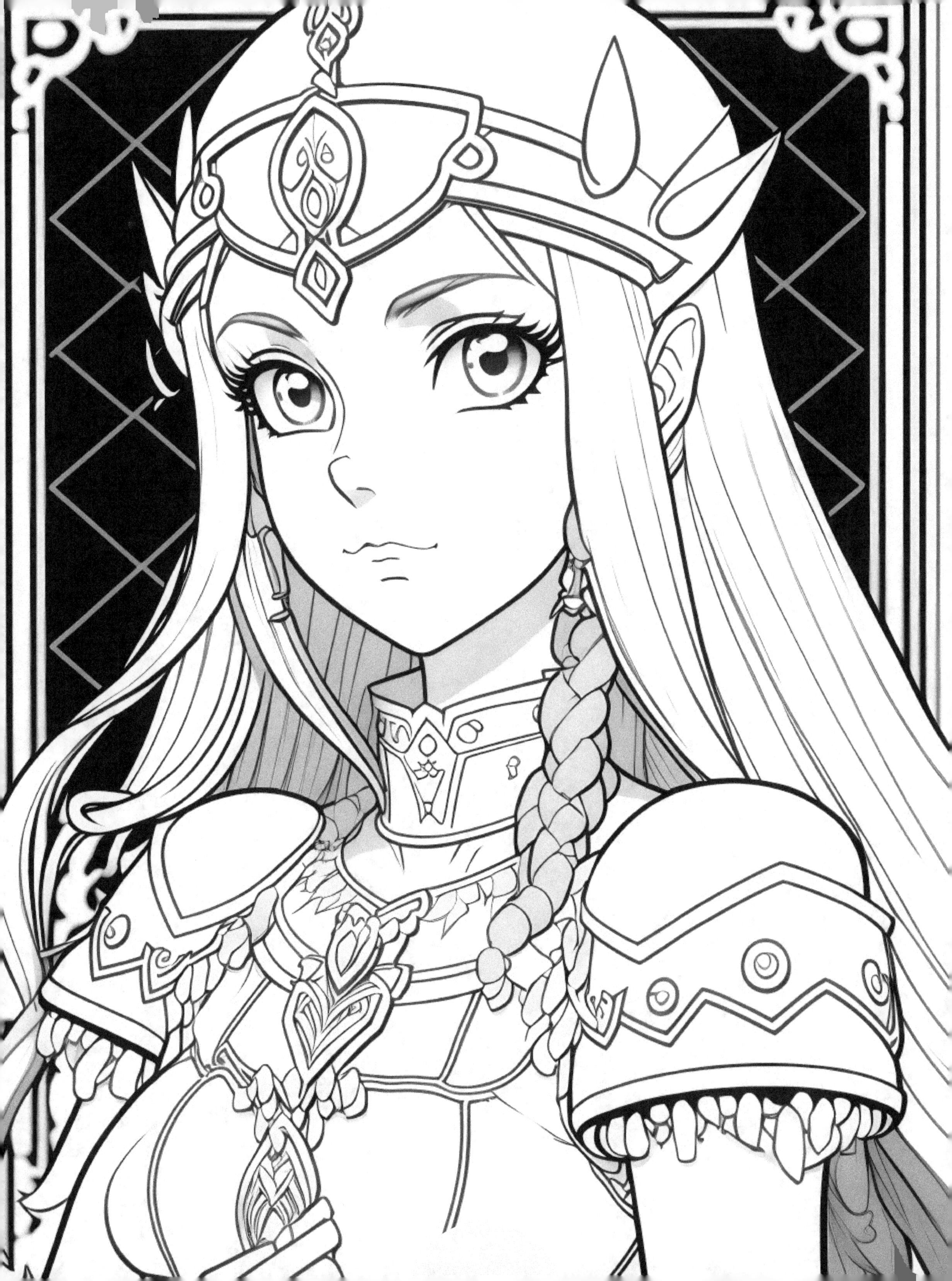

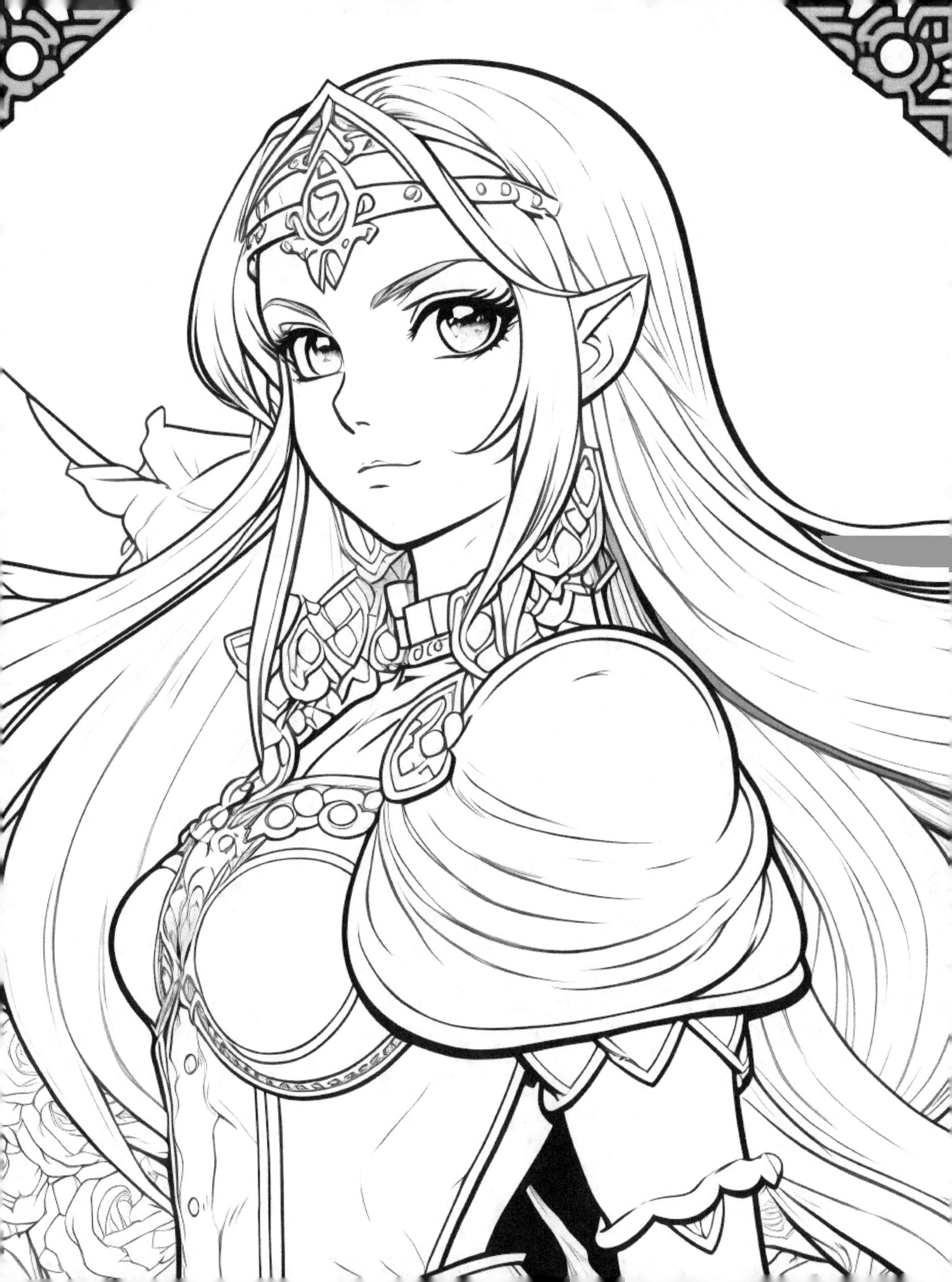

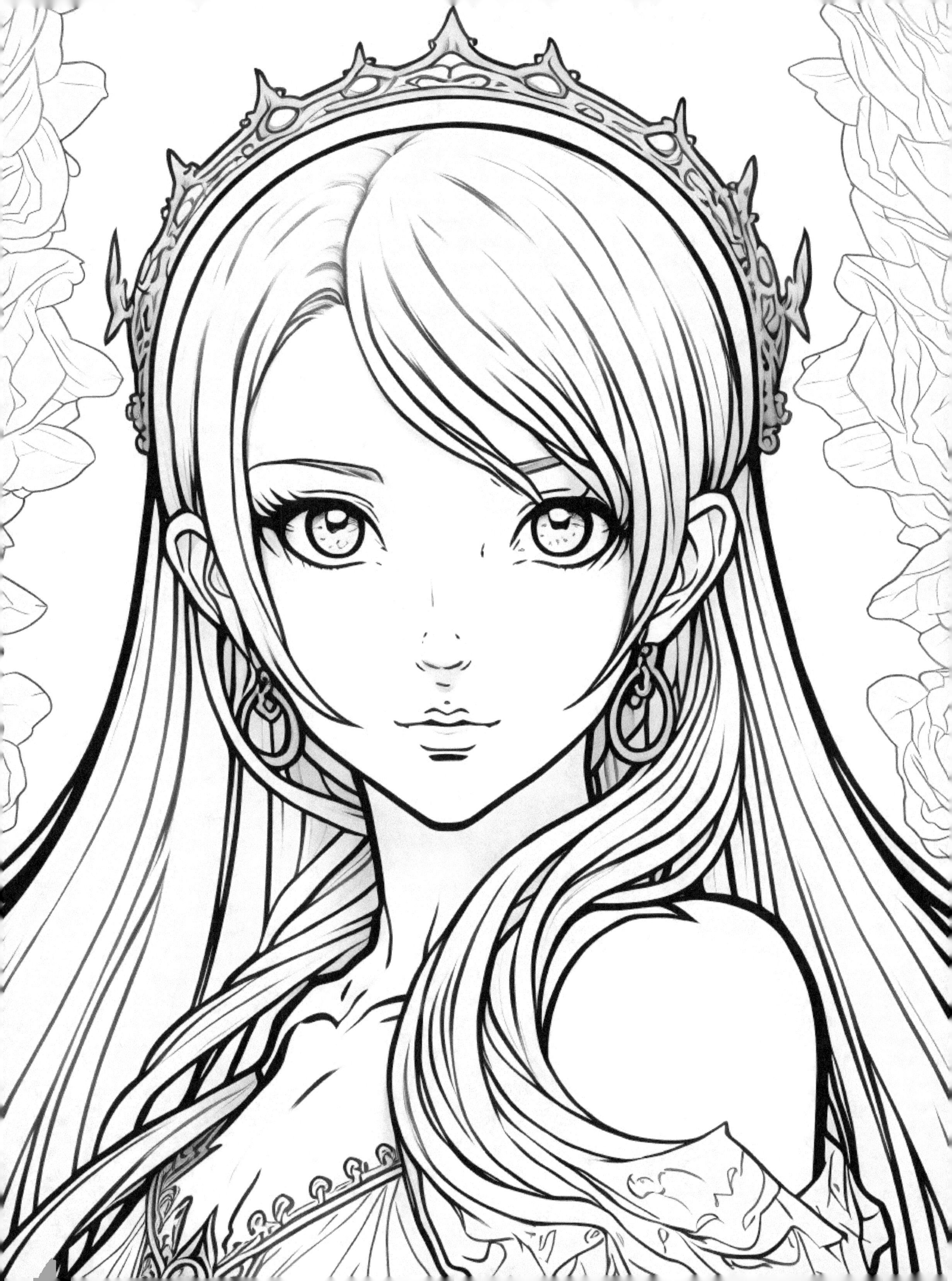

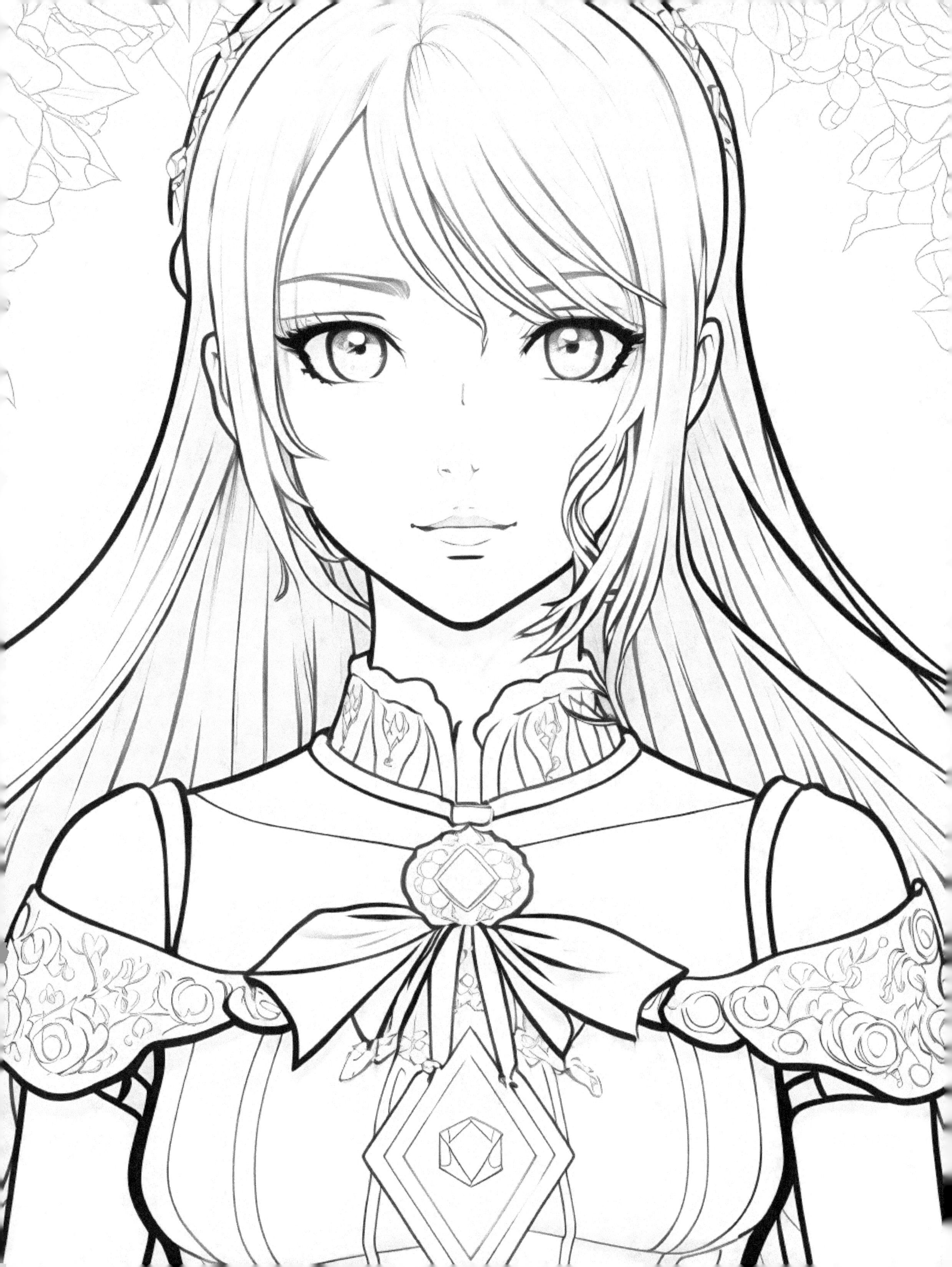

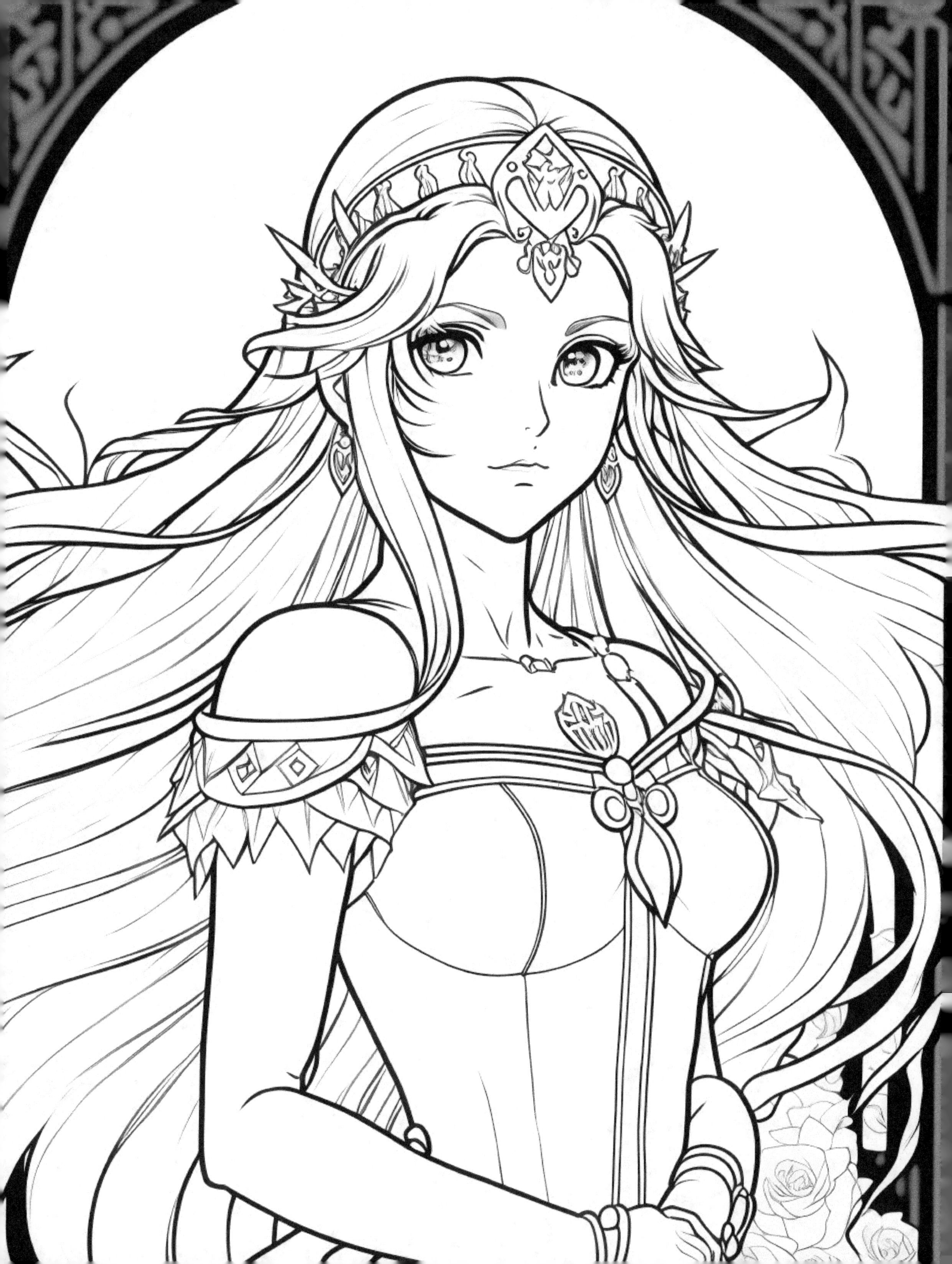

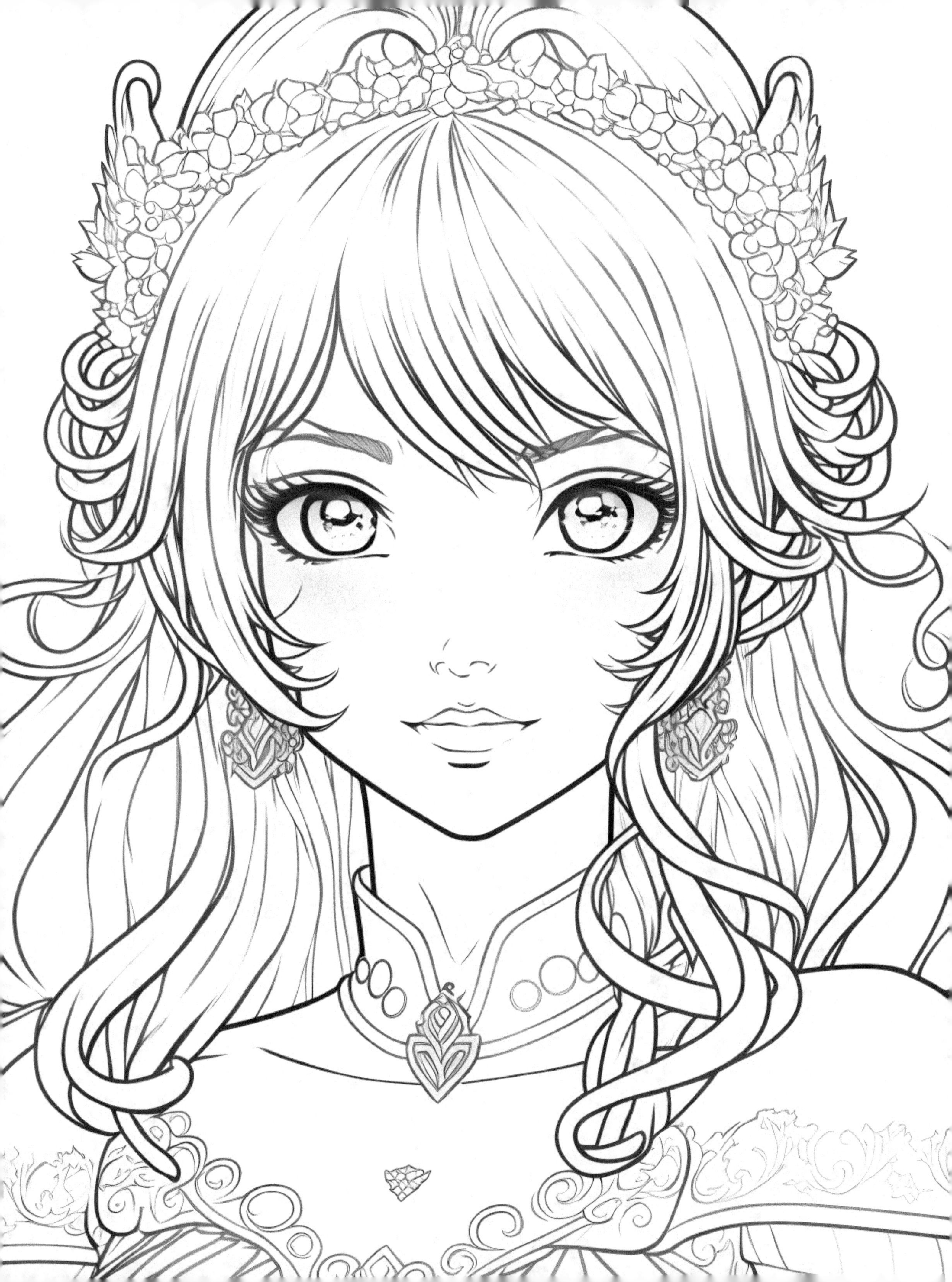

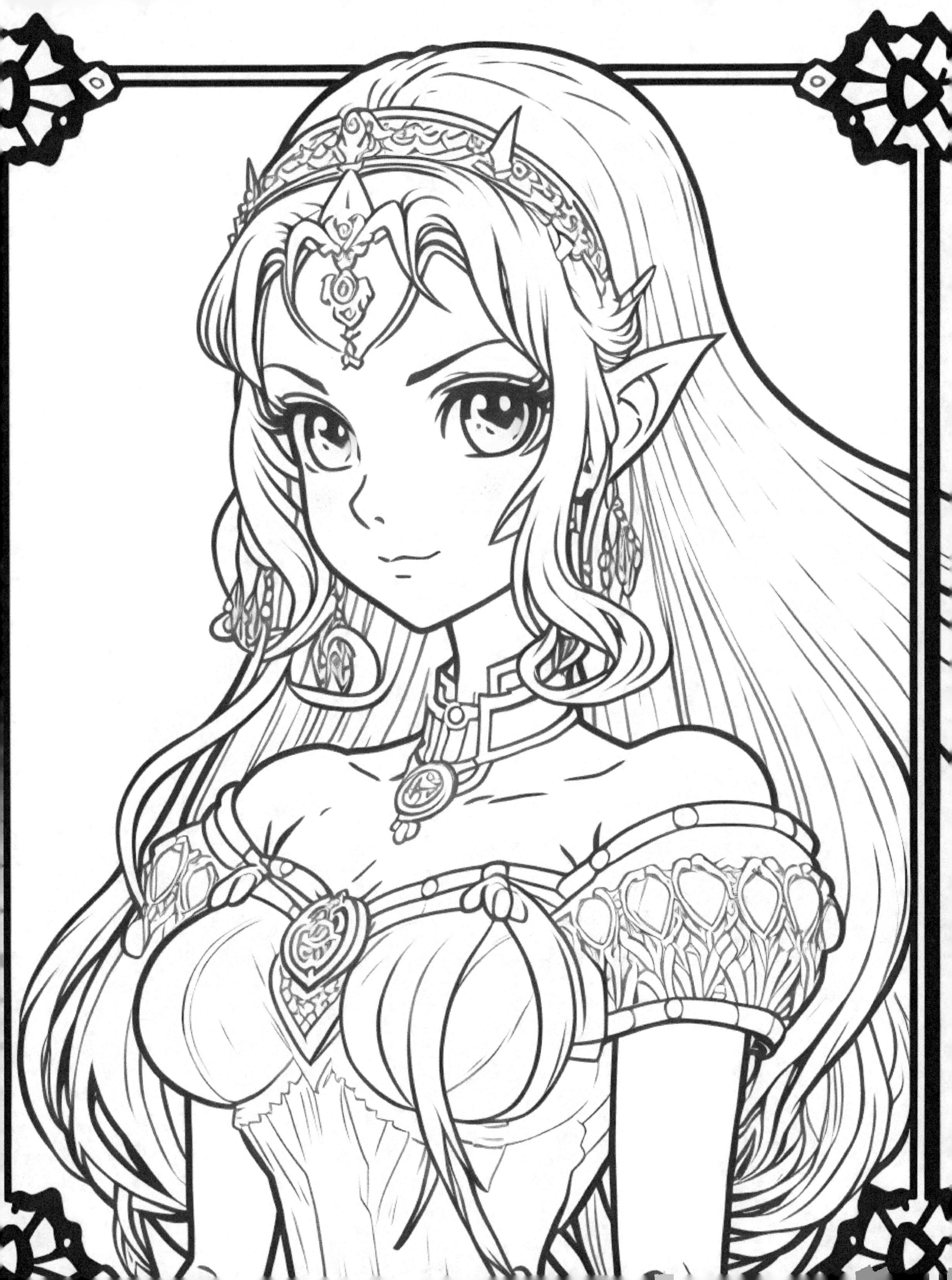

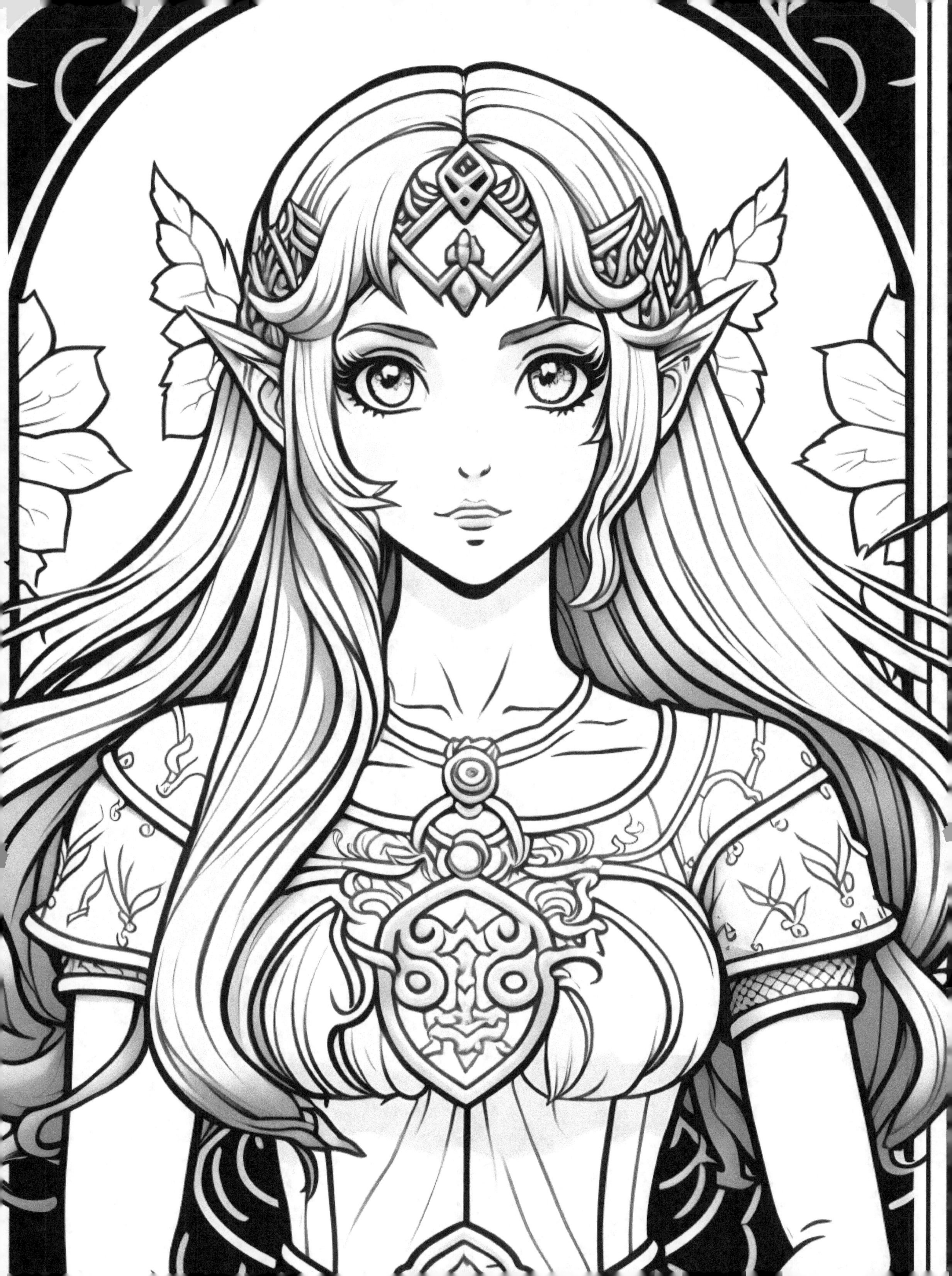

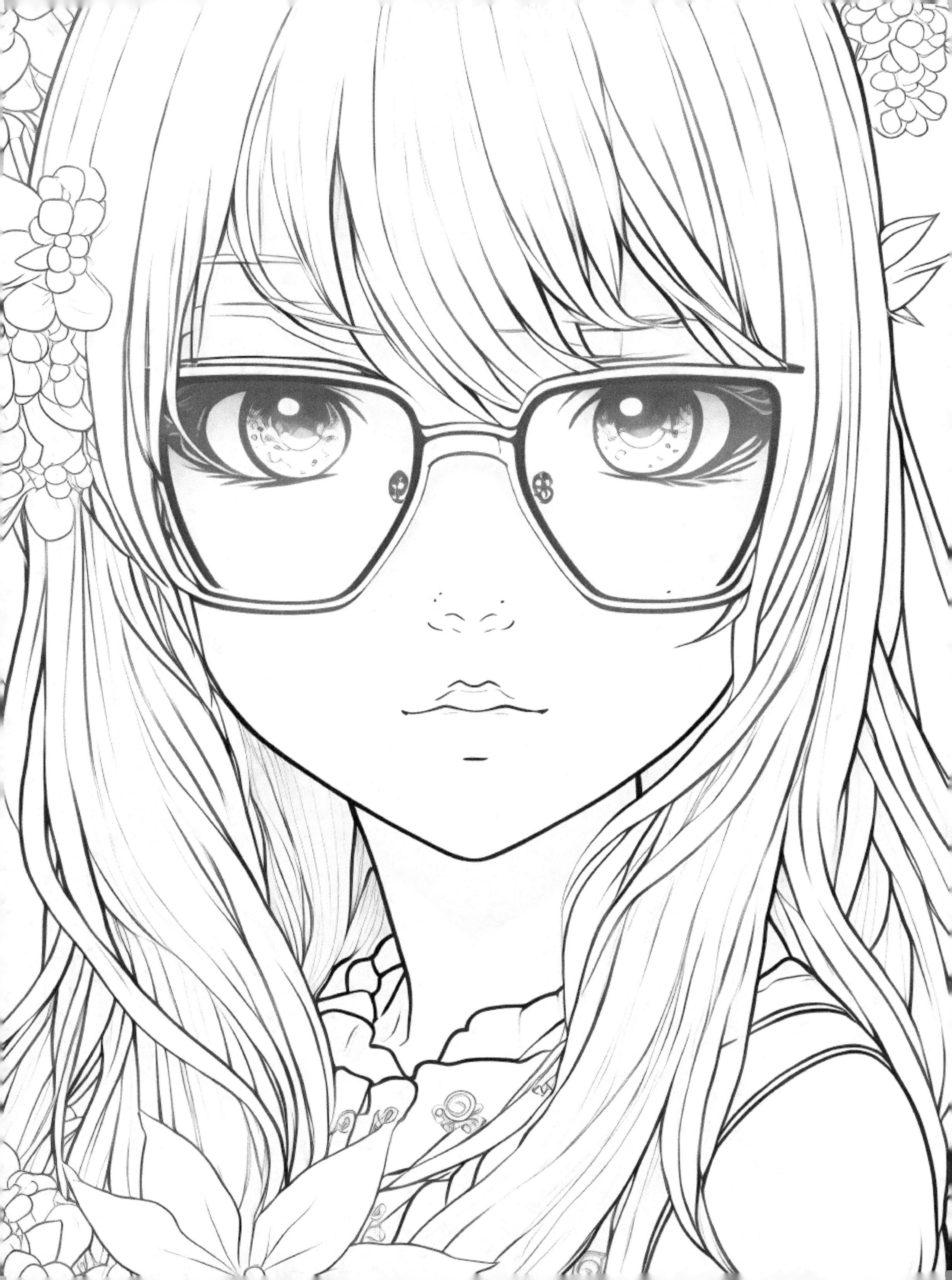

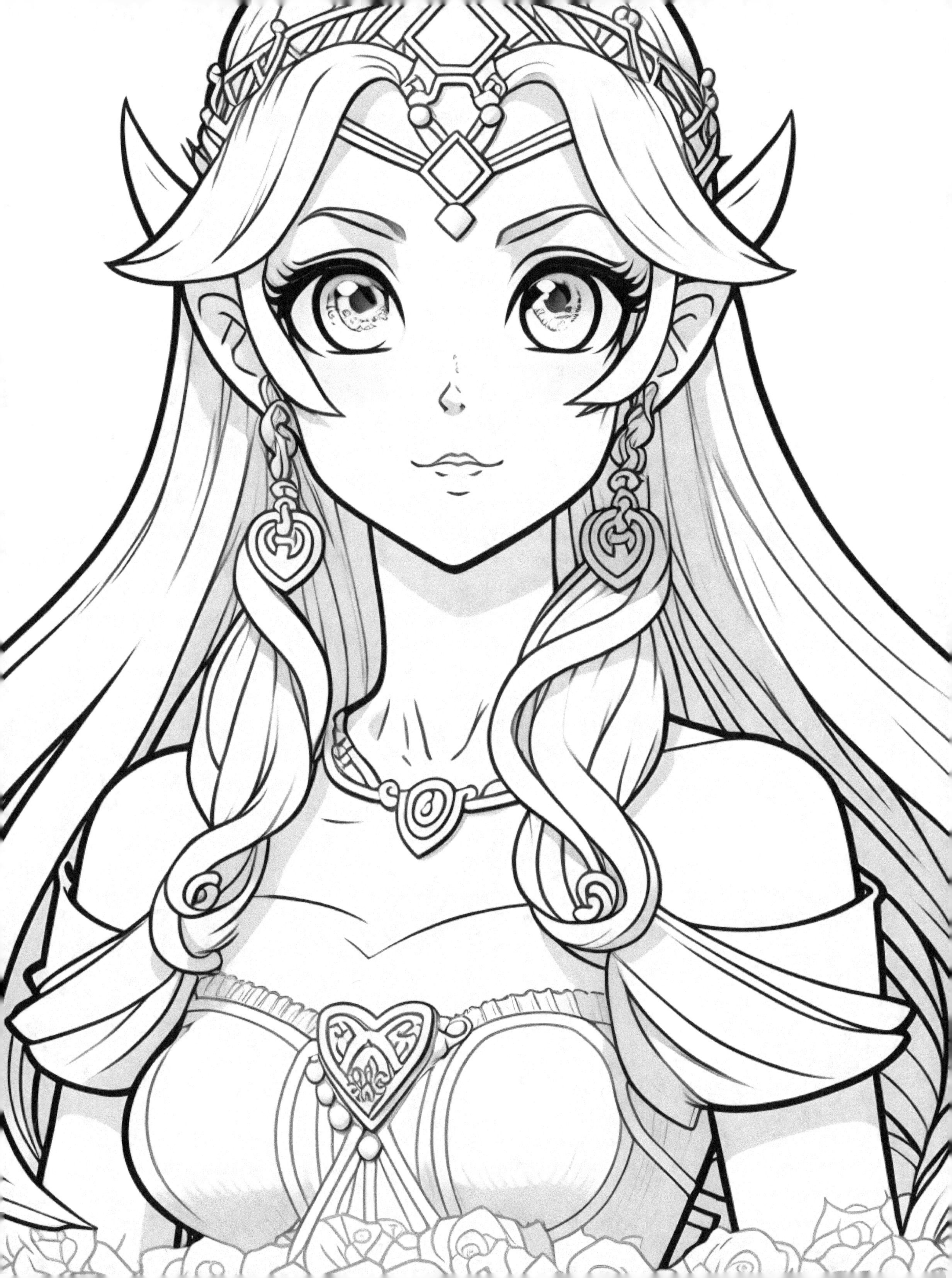

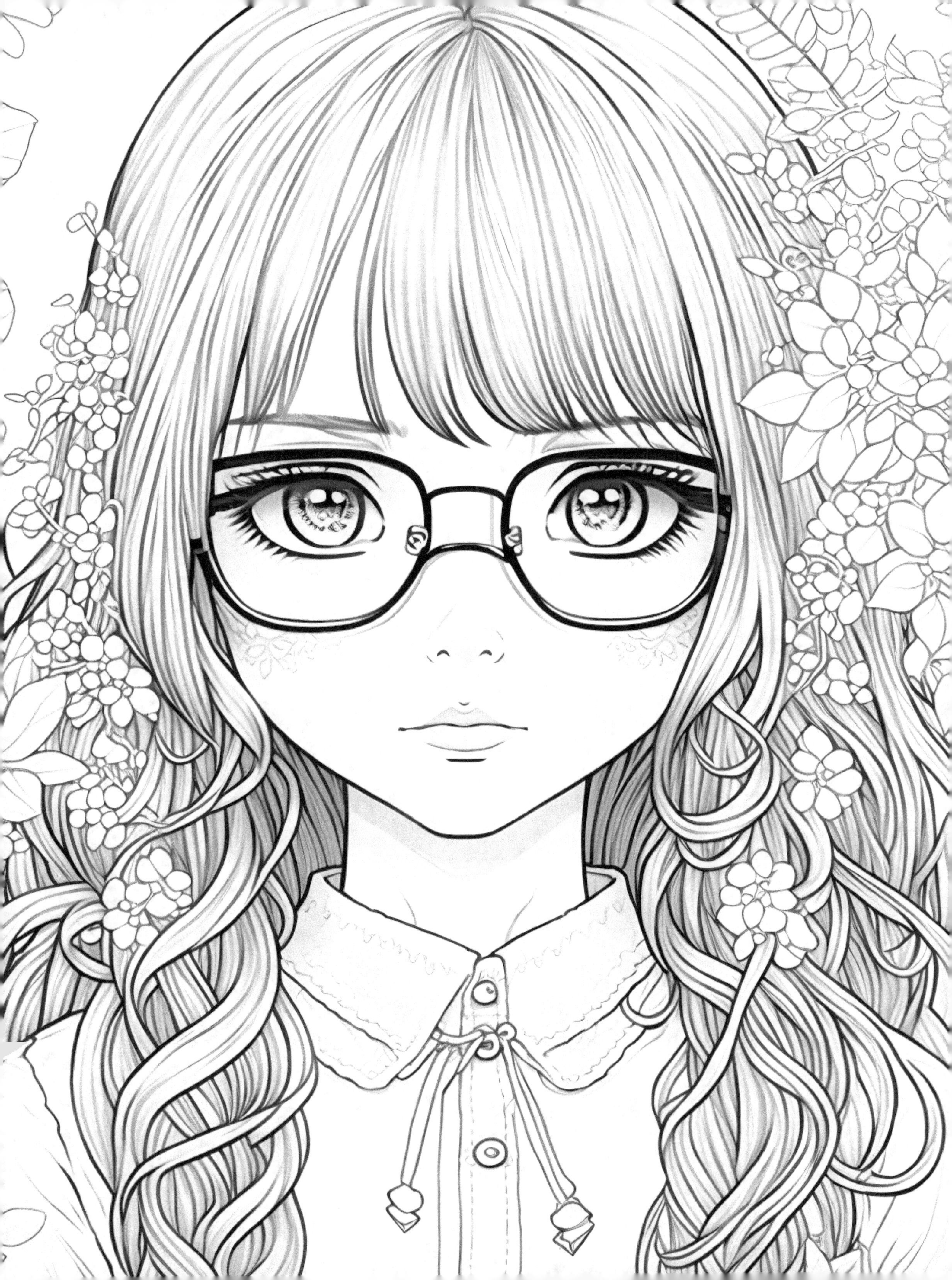

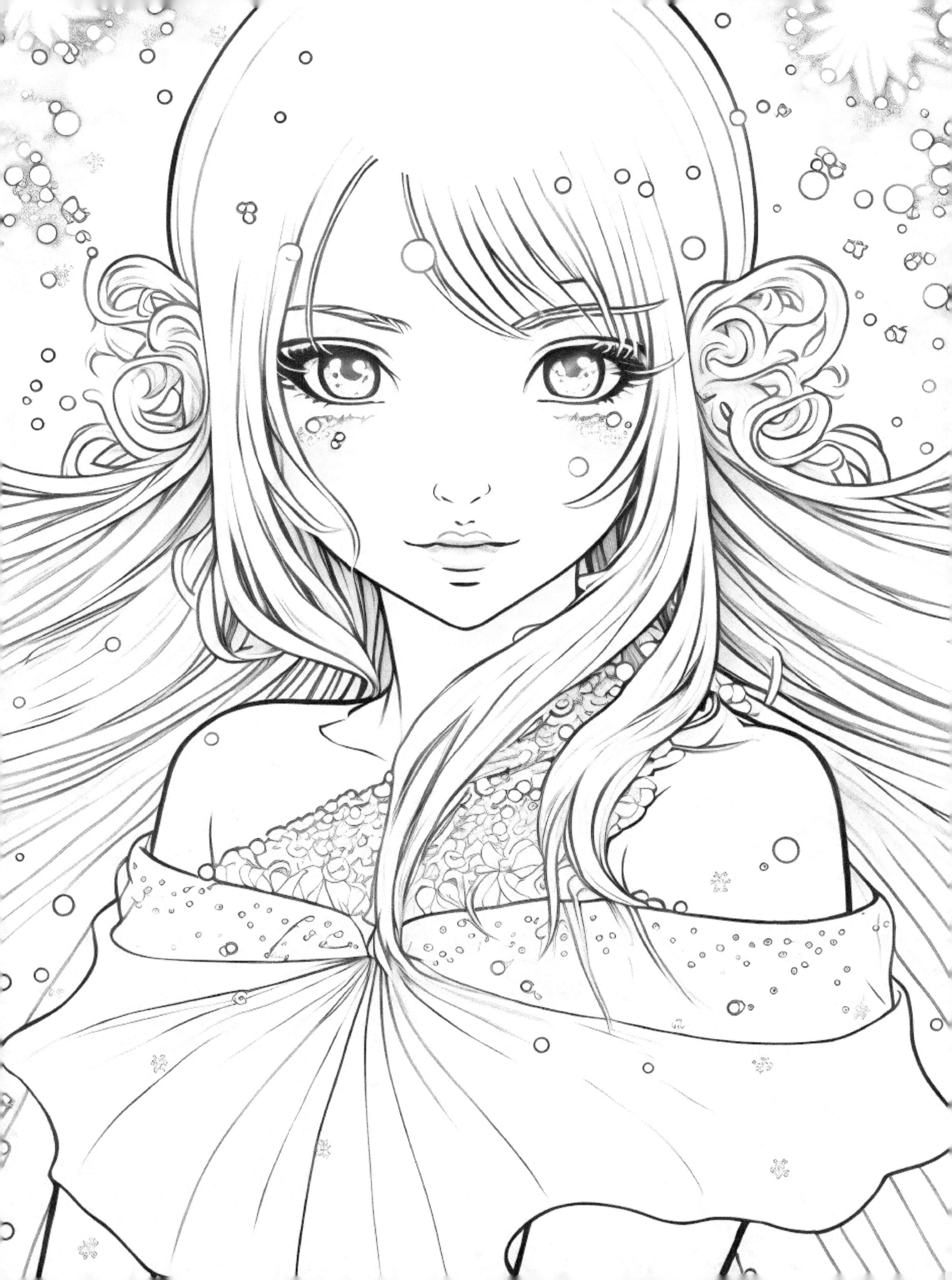

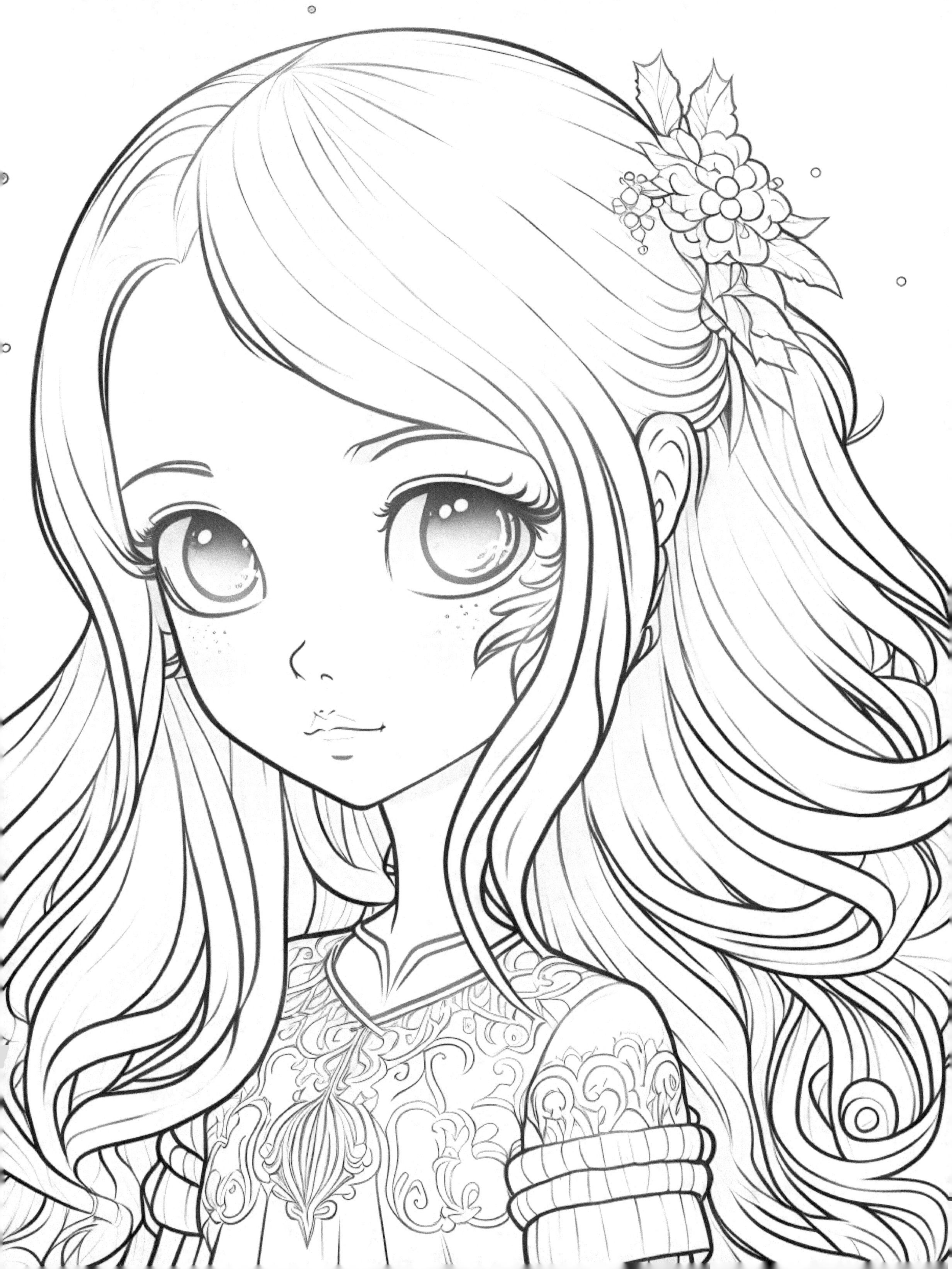

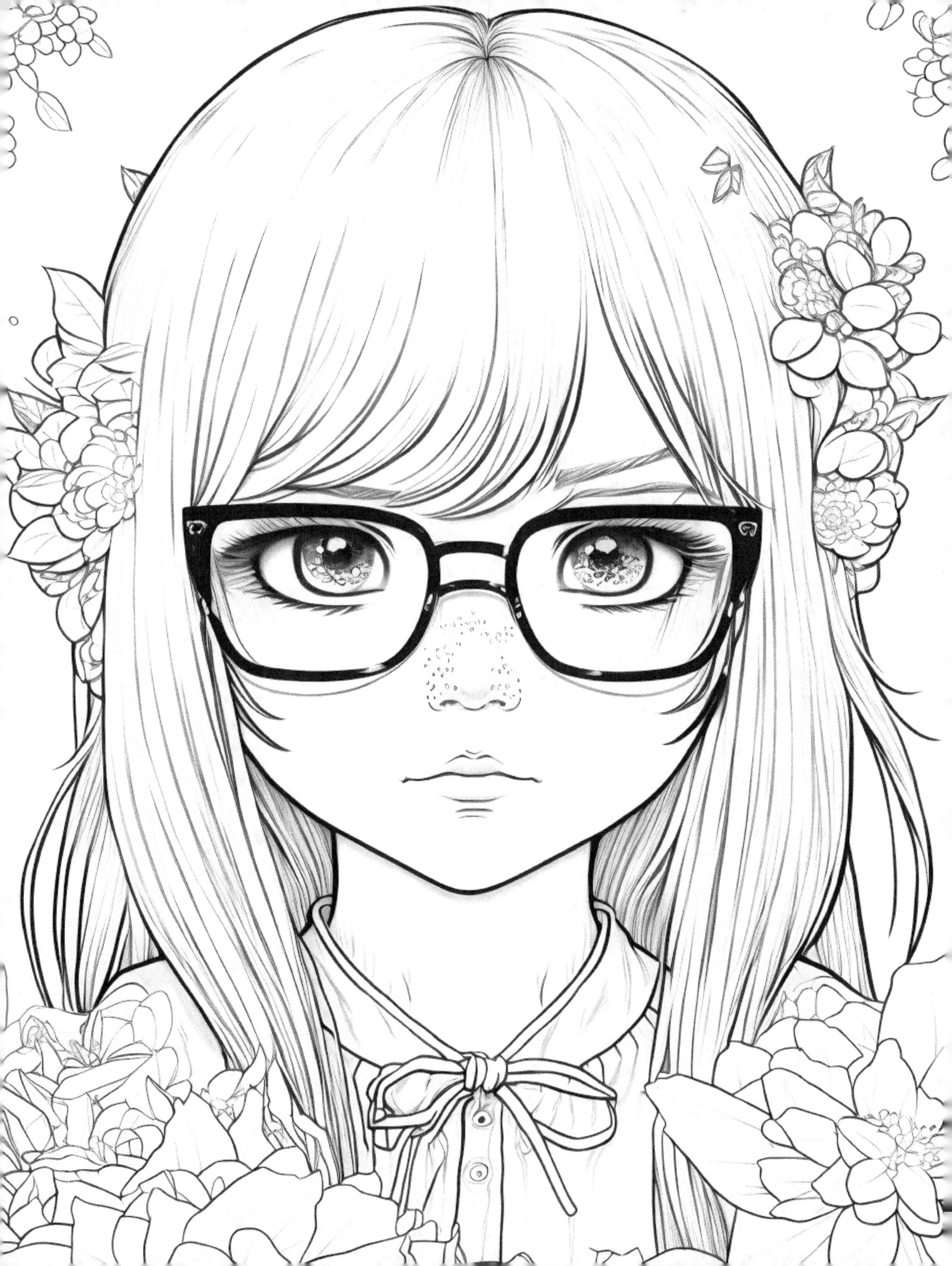

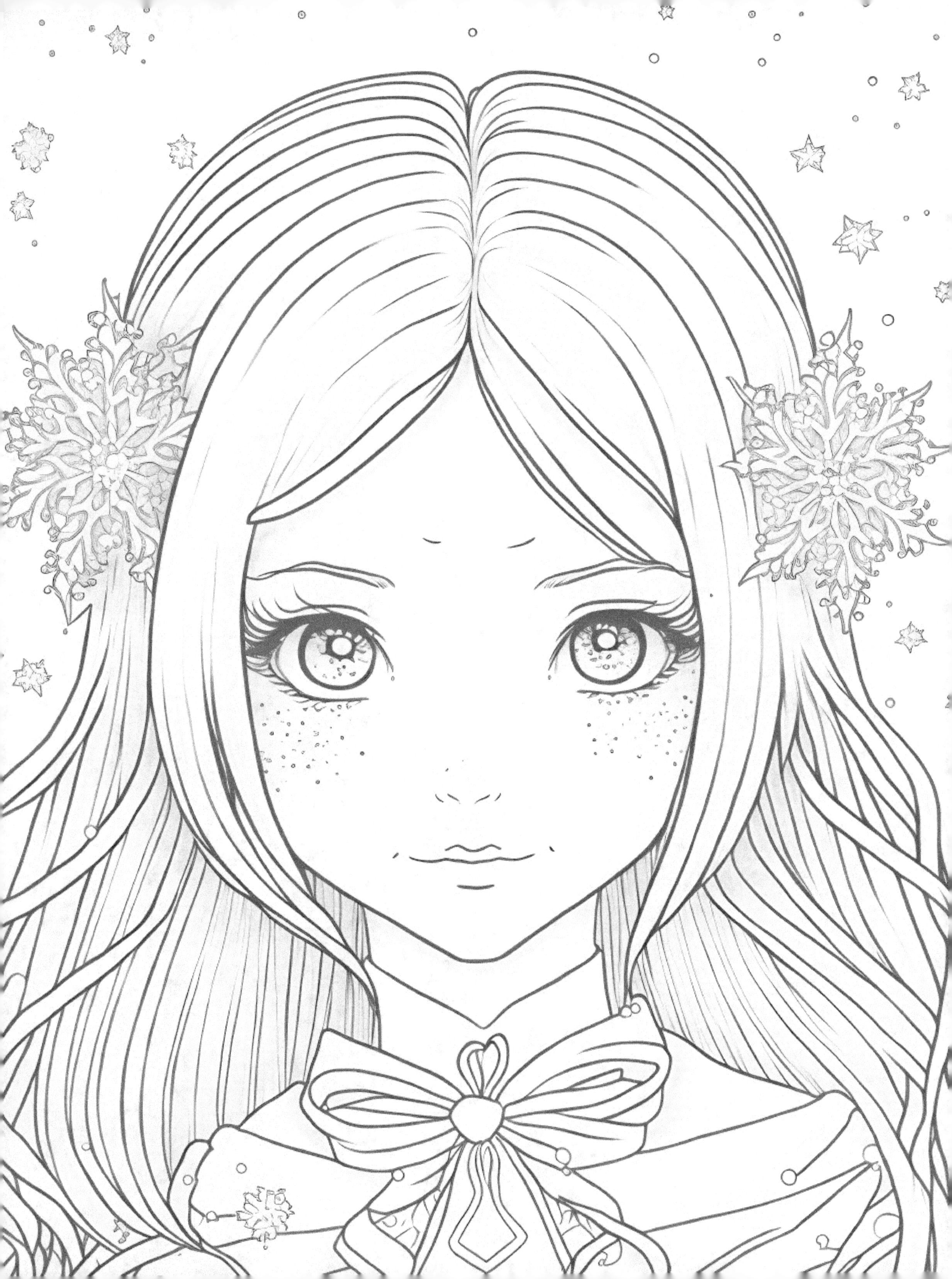

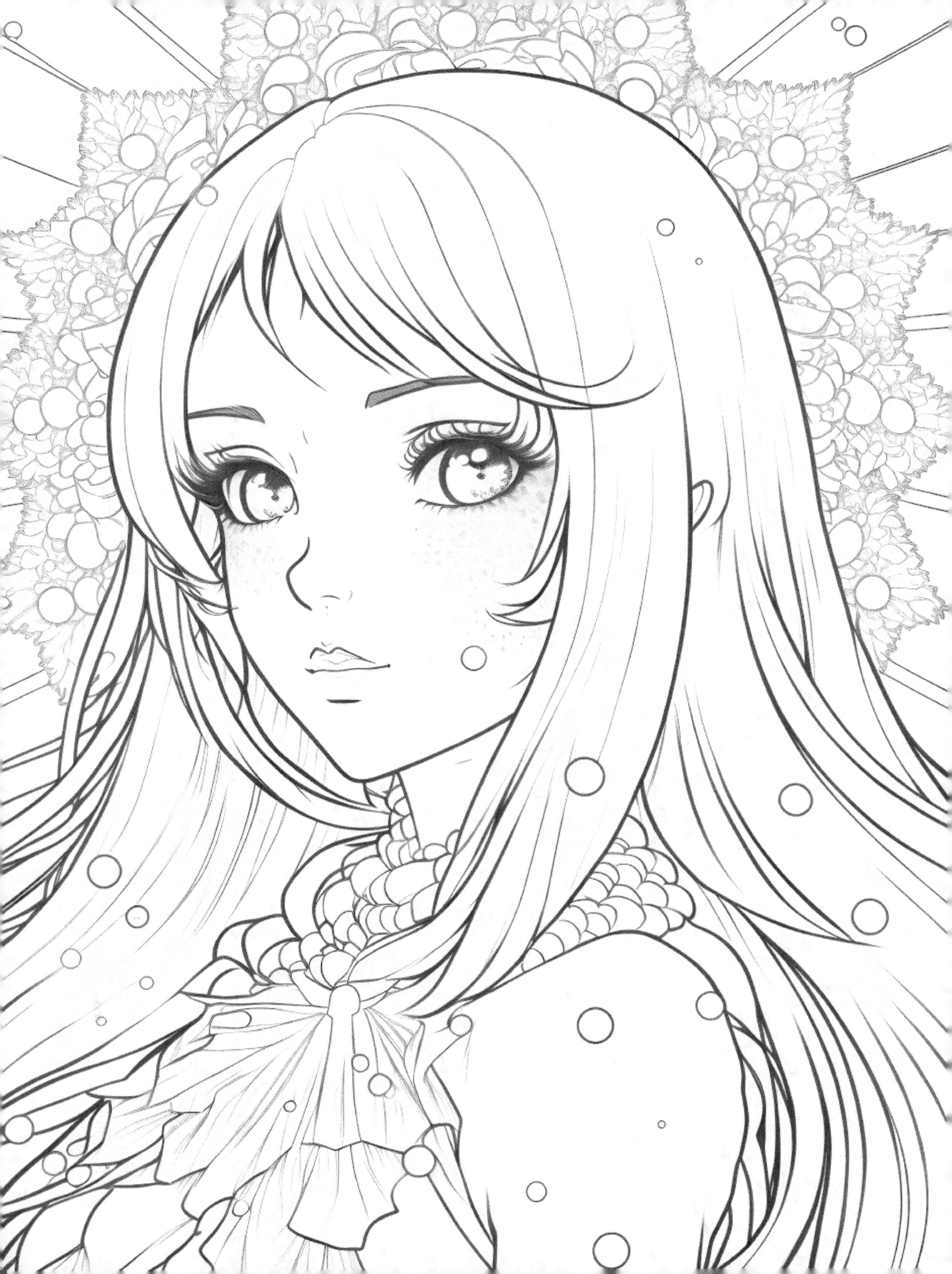

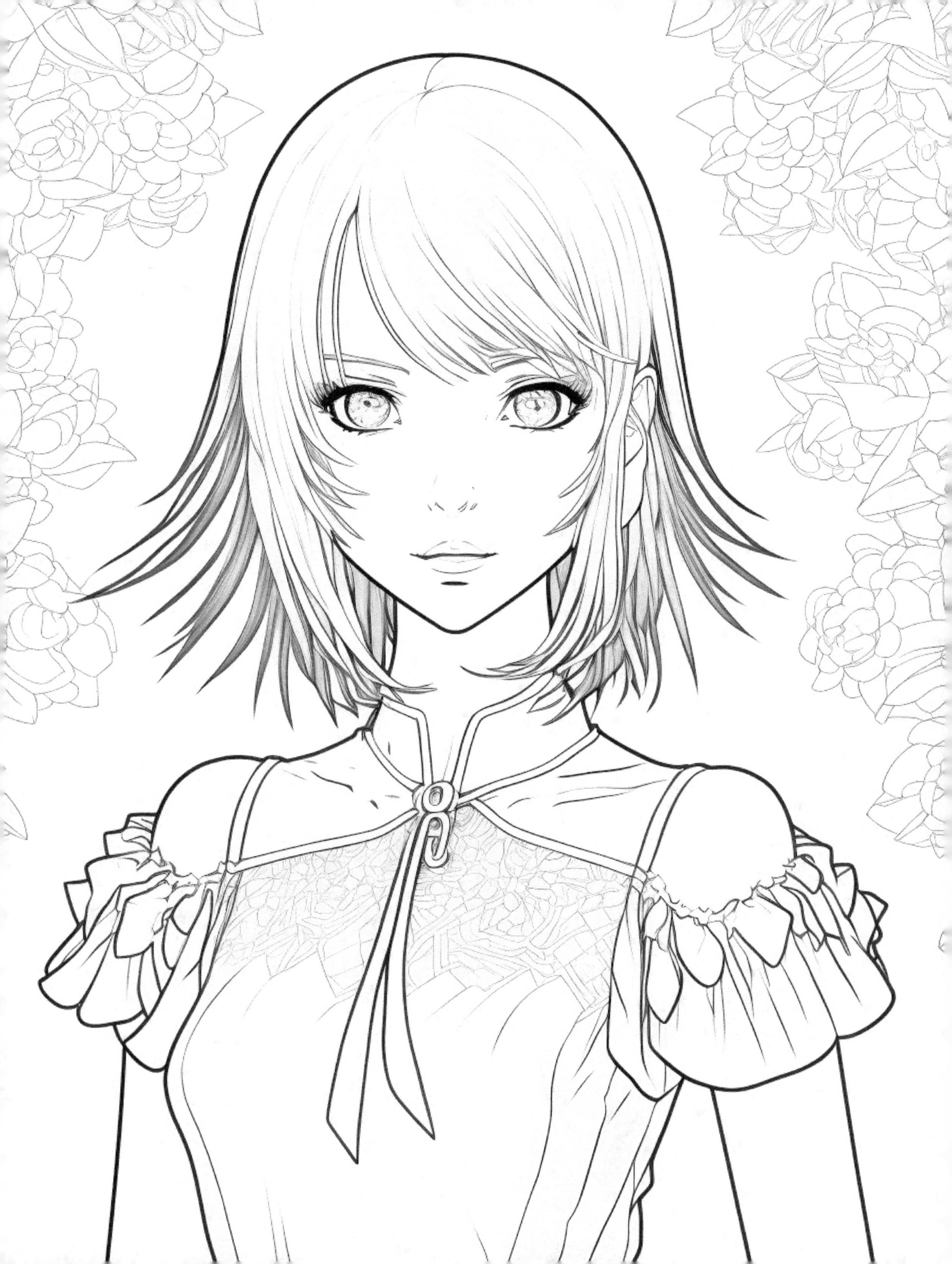

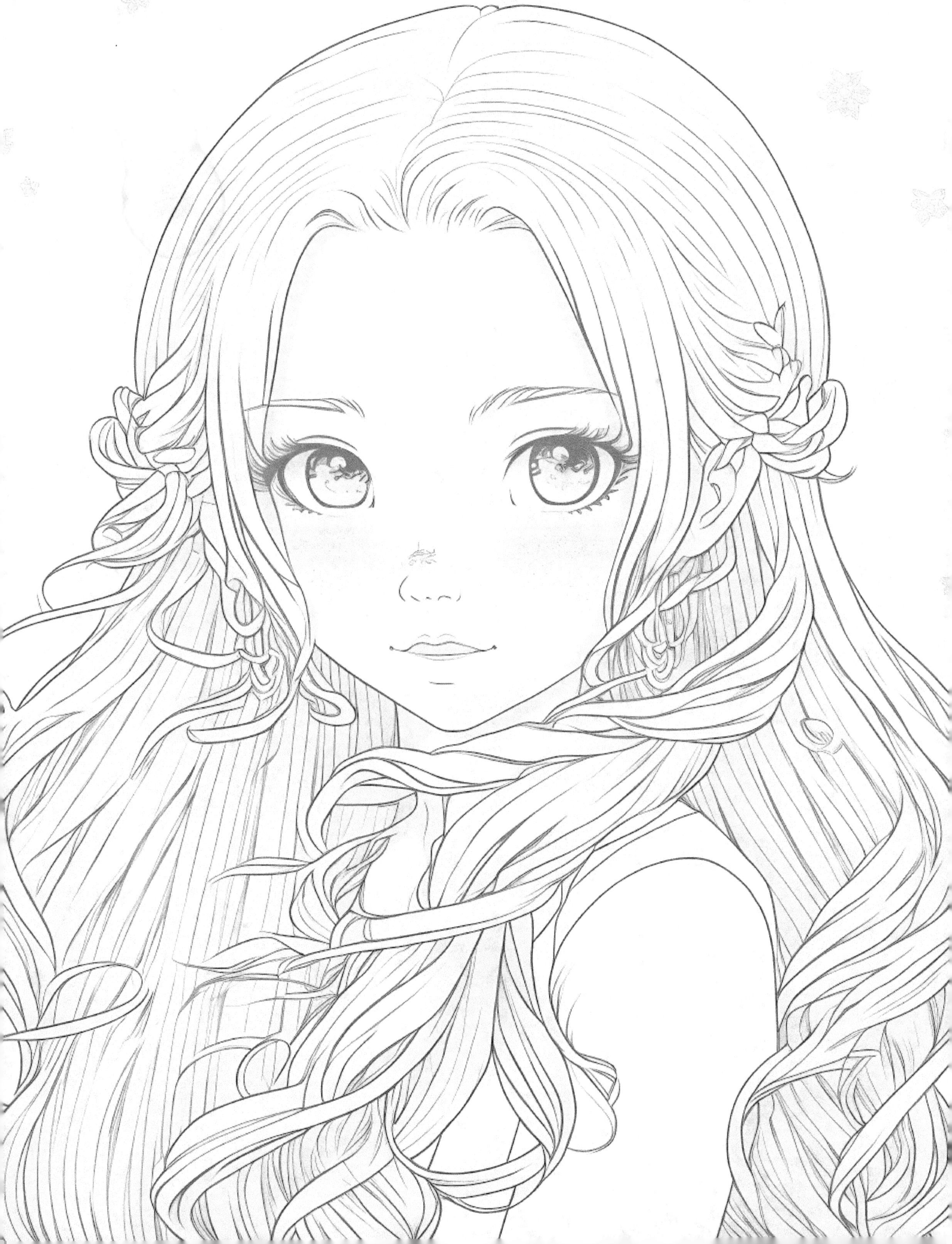

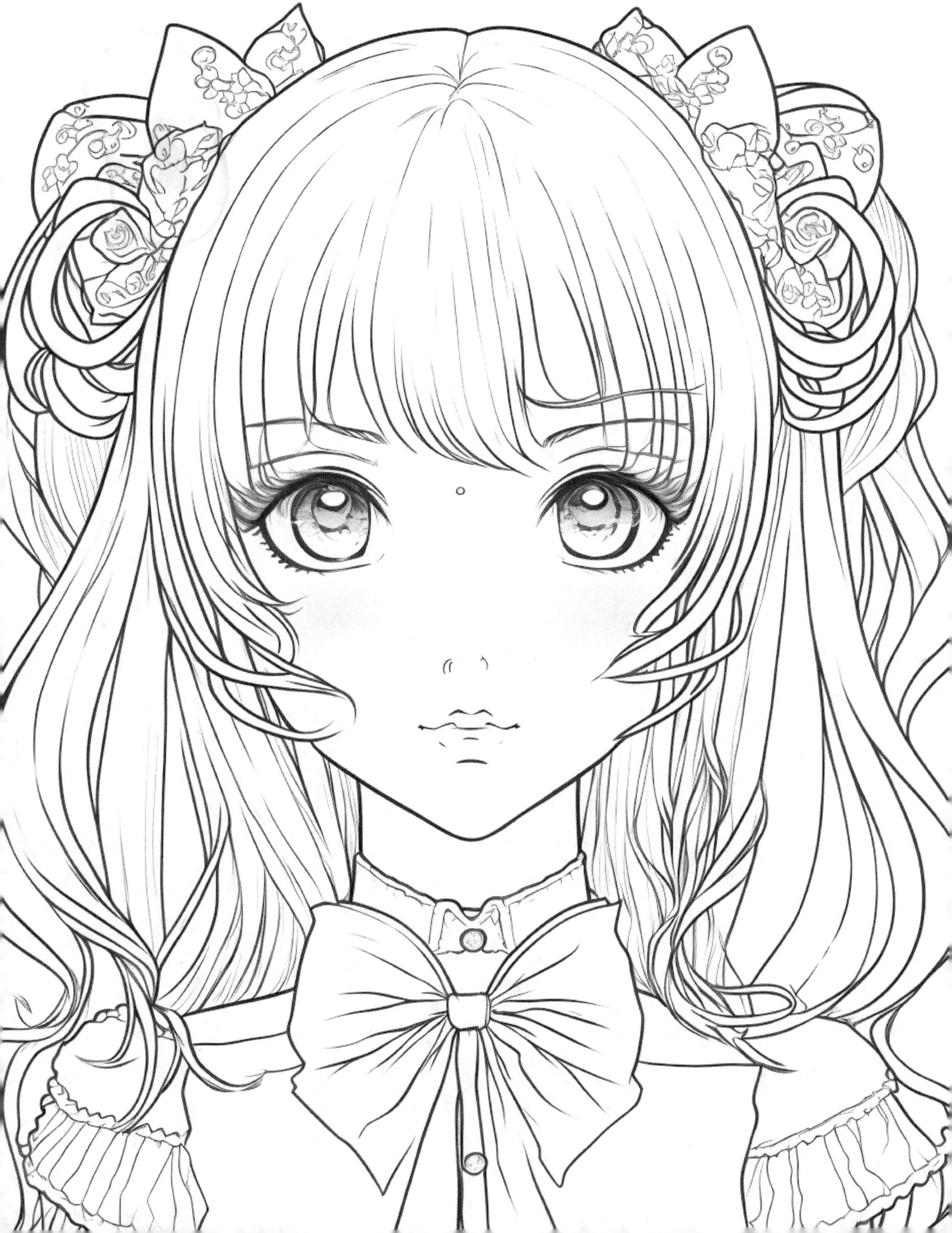

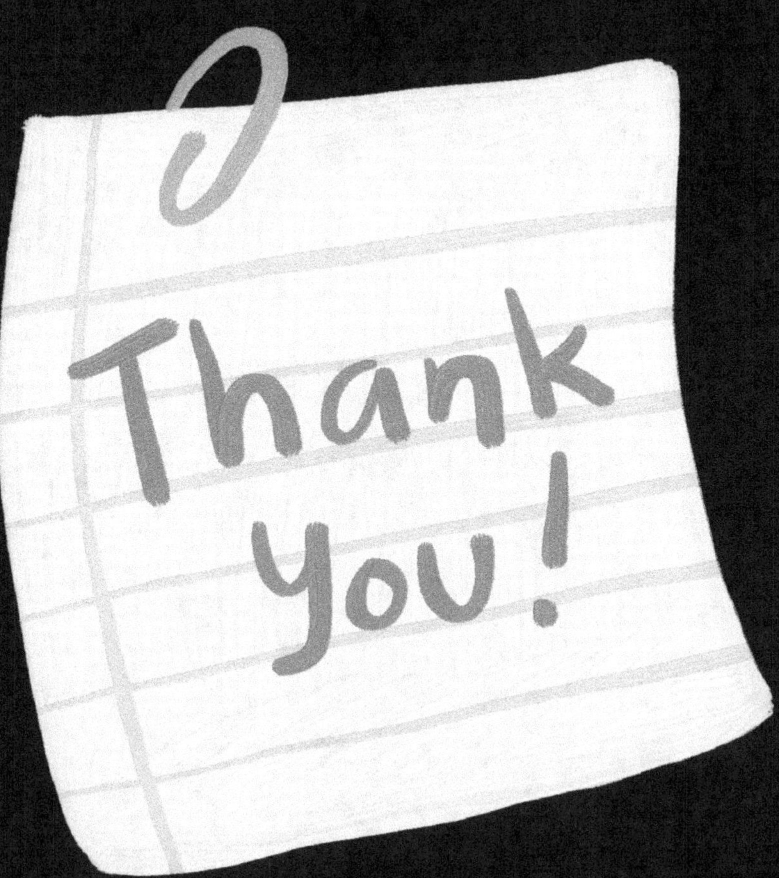

塗り絵 MORE SUPER KAWAII PRINCESSES

CAPI CAMP
ESTUDIOS

www.ingramcontent.com/pod-product-compliance
Lightning Source LLC
Chambersburg PA
CBHW081626220526
45467CB00029B/3165
* 9 7 9 8 3 8 9 3 3 1 3 8 9 *